THE
COPYWRITING
SOURCEBOOK

ANDY MASLEN

THE COPYWRITING SOURCEBOOK

**HOW TO WRITE BETTER COPY,
FASTER — FOR EVERYTHING FROM
ADS TO WEBSITES**

mc Marshall Cavendish
Business

Copyright © 2010 Andy Maslen

First published in 2010 by Marshall Cavendish Business
An imprint of Marshall Cavendish International

PO Box 65829
London EC1P 1NY
United Kingdom

and

1 New Industrial Road
Singapore 536196
genrefsales@sg.marshallcavendish.com
www.marshallcavendish.com/genref

Marshall Cavendish is a trademark of Times Publishing Limited

Other Marshall Cavendish offices: Marshall Cavendish International (Asia) Private Limited,
1 New Industrial Road, Singapore 536196 • Marshall Cavendish Corporation. 99 White
Plains Road, Tarrytown NY 10591–9001, USA • Marshall Cavendish International (Thailand)
Co Ltd. 253 Asoke, 12th Floor, Sukhumvit 21 Road, Klongtoey Nua, Wattana, Bangkok
10110, Thailand • Marshall Cavendish (Malaysia) Sdn Bhd, Times Subang, Lot 46, Subang
Hi-Tech Industrial Park, Batu Tiga, 40000 Shah Alam, Selangor Darul Ehsan, Malaysia

A CIP record for this book is available from the British Library

ISBN 978-0-462-09974-3

Designed by www.stazikerjones.co.uk
Index prepared by Indexing Specialists (UK) Ltd

Printed and bound in Singapore by Times Printers Pte Ltd

Contents

Acknowledgements

Many people have inspired, helped and encouraged me to write this book and this is my chance to repay them. First, as always, my clients, a great group of people to write for and without whose commissions I wouldn't have gained much copywriting experience at all.

In particular, I'd like to thank those individuals who graciously allowed me to quote from, and in some cases reproduce, their marketing campaigns: Paul Joyce, Marketing Director, William Reed Business Media; Santa Marku, Head of Product Marketing, BSI; Paul Lewis, Head of Public Relations, RSPB; Nigel Jagger, Chairman, Cert Octavian plc; Kevin Harrington, Director, Sodexo; John Harrison, Streetwise Publications; James Phillips, Managing Director, Lewis Direct Mail; Sally Bibb, Director, talentsmoothie; James Evelegh, Editor, InPublishing; Clair Darke, Marketing Manager, FAST Ltd; James Kelly, Managing Director, Lorien Resourcing and Peter Clay, co-founder, crocus.co.uk

Martin Liu, Pom Somkabcharti and the team at Marshall Cavendish have, once again, offered invaluable advice in the most generous spirit. Ross Speirs, my friend and creative partner, is another source of advice on all matters design-related, and much else besides. Jane Kingsmill, Richard Harrison and Jane Bainbridge are all friends, and writers: they've shared their thoughts on email and web writing and the correct approach for articles.

Jo Maslen is my wife and Commercial Director of Sunfish. Over the last 12 years, we've bounced around hundreds if not thousands of ideas on the best way to write copy for different pieces. And, finally, my sons, Rory and Jacob, who always provide a dazzlingly different perspective on the world and remind me that there's more to life than writing headlines.

Thank you all.

For my parents, the first to show me the power of words to move hearts and minds

INTRODUCTION

I remember my first ever copywriting job. It was 1986 and I had to write a sales letter. All I remember was my panic at having to fill two sides of A4 with selling copy... before lunchtime.

What I would have given for some simple guidelines on what to include, how to structure it and what style to adopt. I guess that memory was behind my idea for The Copywriting Sourcebook.

You don't need to read the whole book – or not in one go anyway – just turn to the chapter that deals with the marketing piece you're writing now.

Over the next couple of hundred pages or so, I give you step-by-step advice and templates for 12 of the most common copywriting tasks, plus a separate chapter focusing on headlines. I've drawn on my experience writing copy both in corporate marketing roles and, since 1996, as an independent copywriter working for hundreds of different clients all over the world.

You get explicit, practical, step-by-step guidelines that help you write better copy, faster, for a wide range of formats, both online and offline. I help you answer the big questions we all face as copywriters:

- How do I write copy that works in any format?
- How do I adapt copy from print to digital communications?
- What is the best way to set out any type of sales or marketing piece?
- How can I save time when writing copy under pressure?

And what of the Internet? I have argued in the past that good copy works wherever you put it. That's true at the conceptual level, but there are differences between the web and print and I explore them in the chapters on emails, e-zines, AdWords and web pages.

Seven ways this book helps you

1. Helps you achieve sales, marketing and commercial goals.
2. Gives you easy-to-follow advice on the right way to write copy.
3. Provides real-world examples of different copywriting styles and tones of voice.
4. Allows you to write better copy, faster.
5. Takes the stress out of planning and writing any type of marketing or sales copy.
6. Shows you proven shortcuts for beginnings, middles and ends.
7. Explains how a professional copywriter goes about his work.

CHAPTER 1
HEADLINE

FINALLY, THE SIMPLE WAY TO WRITE GREAT HEADLINES

Headlines are so important I think they deserve a chapter to themselves. And they're everywhere: subject lines, envelope messages, banner ads, landing pages, book titles, training course titles. Although most copywriters will tell you they find writing headlines the hardest part of any job, sometimes they just seem to arrive out of the ether. One of my own favourites in this category is from a subscriptions renewal letter I wrote for *Top Gear* magazine. The headline reads:

> People who think dolphins are cleverer than McLaren engineers want to ruin your fun

The letter was signed by Jeremy Clarkson, the lead presenter for the *Top Gear* TV programme, who also has a monthly column in the magazine. It captures his trademark tone of voice and style and does, I think, contain a clear appeal to the reader's self-interest. Namely, not having their enjoyment of cars spoiled by do-gooders. How long did it take me to write? There are three answers. One, about 15 seconds, the time it took me to type it out. Two, about five minutes, daydreaming about fast cars. Or three, 35 years, which was the time I'd spent watching *Top Gear* on the television and internalising the brand values of the show (and, latterly, the spin-off magazine).

However, that was a rarity. Most of the time, I'm like all the rest, sweating over headlines, finally coming up with a good one, then paralysed by fear that as I send it off to a client, maybe one of the rejects would have outperformed it. In the end you just have to step up to the plate and swing. It might work, it might not, but you can't second-guess your list.

So let me ask you a question. What do you think is the purpose of the headline? Here are a few possible answers:

a) to demonstrate to the reader how clever I am
b) to indulge my taste for wordplay and 'humour'
c) to stop the reader from turning the page
d) to make the reader want to read the body copy

e) to encapsulate my sales pitch in 10-16 words or fewer

f) to fit in with the picture I have chosen

g) to allow me to use the same tired old cliché as our competitors

h) to raise brand awareness

Though they would never admit it, many copywriters – both in-house and agency/freelance – are clearly motivated by a combination of a), b), f), g) and h). This type of writer frequently, though not always, works in an above-the-line role, where measuring results from specific executions or campaigns is difficult if not impossible. (But grinning broadly as they drive by a 96-sheet poster with their headline on it is effortless if not mandatory.) Writers working below-the-line, where everything is measurable (and testable) tend to opt for a combination of c), d) and e). (Though not always.)

Winning the battle for eyeballs

If you need to make money from your marketing campaigns, your headline is your first and biggest weapon in the battle for eyeballs. Get it right and you have a (temporarily) captive audience and the possibility of winning orders. Get it wrong and you have a funny picture for your office wall.

So where do we start? You can roughly divide headlines into three categories:

1. Those promising news.

2. Those arousing curiosity.

3. Those offering a benefit.

When Ogilvy & Mather tested headlines, they found that benefits out-pulled news, which out-pulled curiosity. A combination of all three was the most responsive of all. This is bad news for writers who favour headlines like this:

Have you discovered Acme toner cartridges yet?

Your headline is your first and biggest weapon in the battle for eyeballs.

(Reader: 'No.' Turns page.)

But excellent news for writers who like lines like this:

Fighter pilots: how this everyday vegetable can help you see better at night

(Unfortunately, I'll never use that one, but you get the idea!)

This should be simple then. After all, you know your product inside out, don't you? You know what it does for your customers. You know what makes it special and different. All you have to do is get all that across in a dozen or so words. Oh yes. That. That's what makes writing good headlines so infernally hard.

In case of emergency, break glass

If you find yourself staring into space for more than ten minutes, it's time for emergency action. You're busy. You have too many other things to do to be just sitting there. Here's a way to get something down on paper. It might not be your final line but it will free the wheels and let you get on with the rest of your copy.

Step one: Complete this sentence: My product helps my customers because it…
E.g. My product helps my customers because it saves them money when they buy their next new car.
Step two: Cut everything up to and including 'it'.
E.g. Saves them money when they buy their next new car.
Step three: change 'them' and 'they' to 'you' (and tweak the rest as necessary)
E.g. Save money when you buy your next new car.
Step four: Add 'NOW: an easy way to' at the beginning.
E.g. NOW: an easy way to save money when you buy your next new car.

Not bad. Could be better of course. But this only takes a few minutes. And it will be better, much better, than 90% of the headlines you see around you every day.

Practical help

There are no fixed rules on the best format for headlines. But I've always found that 'How to' headlines work well a lot of the time. Openings like these:

How to save £35 a week on your family's food bill

How to impress even the most sceptical ballroom dancing judge

How to win friends and influence people (oops – sorry, not one of mine!)

If you want to add a sense of newsiness, the simplest trick is to add NOW: at the beginning of any headline. And remember, FREE almost always works well in a headline. Don't be shy in business-to-business (b2b) contexts either. Everyone likes getting free stuff.

Try to keep your headlines as short as you can. Under 16 words is good. Ten is better. (But there are also plenty of examples of control-pulverising headlines longer than either of those numbers.) Remember, you're not trying to write the whole pitch, just enough to get your reader interested. And if you feel drawn to words like 'communication', 'effective' or 'significantly', try 'talking', 'better' or 'much' instead.

As a general rule, headlines should be on a single line, two at a pinch. If you really feel the need to keep going, use a subhead instead. Like this:

How to make the perfect sponge cake every time
Order a trial pack of Wonder Mix today and save 99p

You could even add a lead-in that refers to your target, like this:

Attention all homemakers…
How to make the perfect sponge cake every time
Order a trial pack of Wonder Mix today and save 99p

Design and layout

Headlines look better set in a larger point size than your body copy. But don't go mad. As a general rule for most print and online communications, your headline will tend to shout if it's more than twice the point size of your body copy. (Of course, you may want it to shout.) And don't use ALL CAPS: it makes it harder to read quickly and forces your reader to decode it letter by letter. I think simple sentence case looks best; initial caps force the reader's eye to jump up and down as each new word starts (though there's evidence that initial caps also work well).

Finally, never use full stops at the end of your headlines. They say 'stop' and you don't want your reader to stop, you want them to keep reading. The absence of a full stop implies that the sentence hasn't finished yet and they will keep reading till they find one. Look at a newspaper and see if you can find a headline with a full stop.

A few ideas to keep you going

For new products (or things you want to appear new), start with…
Introducing…
Announcing…
Finally…

At last...
New...
Now...
It's here...
After 10 years...

Use a journalistic headline

The secrets of fine wine collecting revealed
237 ways to cut your tax bill this year
Looks good, smells better: is this the ultimate aftershave?

Use storytelling or editorial techniques

They laughed when I sat down at the piano, but when I started to play (a classic)
He started life on the wrong side of the tracks, now he's running the company
Why Susie had to turn down an offer of marriage

Compare value with price

Want a CEO lifestyle on a part-time salary?

Break the price down into manageable chunks

The car you've always dreamt of, for just £129 a month

Feature the discount

Save £100 when you subscribe to *Copywriter Magazine* by Direct Debit

Provide practical information

The seven steps to a perfect lawn
Do you want to improve your copywriting?
Do you make these mistakes in English? (Another classic)
A simple but delicious chocolate cake recipe
How to drop a dress size in two weeks (without giving up chips)

Style your headline as a quotation or testimonial

'I'd never won anything. Then I joined QuizFriends. Now I drive a new BMW'

'You can make money on the stock market without StockPix. I just wouldn't want to try'

'If you're looking for a reliable food mixer, it has to be the FoodStar 500'

Ask your reader a question

Have you ever wished you could retire early?

Are you ready for a snap customs inspection that could cost your company its life?

What would you do with a million pounds?

Can health and safety be improved in your business?

How much do you know about gardening? Take this simple test

Come in half-way through a sentence

Because there's more to driving than miles per gallon.

Some of the above ideas are my own; others I have adapted from other copywriters, including the excellent John Caples' book, *Tested Advertising Methods*. If you don't already own a copy, buy one. You won't be disappointed.

Summary

Headlines are too important to waste on lame puns or bogus 'Ooh! That's intriguing' teasers. This goes double online, when people are even more impatient. If you do nothing else with your next headline, spell out your main benefit. And remember, if your reader can say 'so what?', it's not a benefit.

CHAPTER 2
SALES LETTER

**DEAR READER,
COPYWRITERS
LIKE US KNOW
SOMETHING MOST
FOLK DON'T**

Introduction

Often called, erroneously, a cover letter, the sales letter is probably the most powerful piece of copywriting ever to have been invented. By its very nature personal (if written properly) it takes your sales pitch directly to each and every one of your prospects. It doesn't have to fight for their attention amid a magazine or newspaper full of more interesting editorial. And you have virtually unlimited space in which to make your case.

It can venture forth unaccompanied by a brochure or flyer and just do its job alone. You can illustrate it with product shots or other relevant images, or go for a plain-looking letter that replicates the look and feel of business correspondence. Or you can make it the star of an all-singing, all-dancing direct mail pack including full colour brochure, order form, reply envelope, sheet of technical data... whatever you like and are willing to pay for.

In essence, though, a sales letter must look like a letter. In other words, it should be personally addressed, it should be personally signed, and it should be designed with the minimum of graphic incursion into the text. It should also use a reasonably ordinary typeface – this is not the place to go looking for wacky fonts. And it should address the reader directly throughout, as if it were written just to them.

And a sales letter should sell. Now maybe the sell in question is 'win sales leads we can follow up later'. Maybe it's a straight 'win new orders'. Either way, once you have your goal in mind, the letter must pursue that goal relentlessly. No deviation, no wavering off course.

Strengths

Sales letters are great for conveying large amounts of information. Perfect for convincing someone to buy from you. They'll want a lot of detail before parting with their cash or bank details, so having the option to go to two, four, six... twelve or thirty-two pages gives you the freedom you need to make every possible sales point, overcome every possible objection, offer independent testimony or evidence that what you say is true and so on. The style you are able to write in allows you to be conversational, which engages the reader more deeply in your message, and means they will read on, past paragraph breaks, page breaks, even separate sheets.

The greatest strength of the sales letter is that it is – or should be – personal. Even in an age when for most people, email or social networking have replaced paper-based correspondence, letters have the power to stop someone in their tracks and make them *read*. The Dear Mr Smith at the beginning and the Yours sincerely, Jane Moore at the bottom mean it *is* a personal communication, despite the fact each reader is one of a group of hundreds, thousands or millions.

> **The greatest strength of the sales letter is that it is – or should be – personal.**

Weaknesses

The greatest weakness of the sales letter is the popular name most recipients give it: 'junk mail'. Although the direct marketing industry (of which I am a part) strives magnificently to popularise the phrase direct mail, this is purely a term of art *within* the business. Punters might refer to 'mailshots' as an alternative, but not in any particularly approving way.

In other words, most recipients of sales letters tend to view them with suspicion if not outright hostility. They suspect, rightly in many cases, that the envelope contains irrelevant promises couched in spammy language.

This puts additional pressure on you as the copywriter to imbue your sales letter with throat-grabbingly immediate relevance to your reader. Your English, while faultless, must also be invisible to your reader; we don't want them noticing our style, just ordering our products.

What can you use it for?

You can use sales letters to communicate with all sorts of groups: members, subscribers, prospects, customers, former customers, customers about to become ex-customers, exhibition visitors, enquirers, website visitors... whomever you have a name and address for. You can use them to...

- Generate enquiries
- Get requests for a white paper or free report
- Push people to your website to get a download
- Send out trial issues of a magazine
- Generate requests for free samples
- Generate requests for a free product or service trial
- Sell additional products or services to existing customers
- Sell upgraded memberships
- Ask for help finding new members – 'member-get-member'
- Ask for awards nominees
- Ask for speakers at a conference or seminar
- Ask for feedback on a soft launch of a new website

What goes wrong?

Boring or clichéd openings
How many direct mail letters have you opened where the writer begins by telling you how they feel? You know the sort of thing...

Dear Mr Smith,

I am delighted to tell you...

Or,

It gives me great pleasure to inform you...

Like we care!

Do not fall into the trap of starting an unsolicited sales letter, which many if not most of the recipients will categorise as 'junk mail', with a statement, however brief, of *your* feelings. The reader must be forgiven for saying, 'I don't know your company, I don't know your products, I don't know you … and you're telling me about your feelings. Now what was it you wanted to talk to me about?'

Nor should you open with a lecture. This style is much loved by copywriters working for any sort of knowledge-based business, such as business or professional information publishing (where I started my career).

The typical letter opens something like this:

Dear Ms Jones,

In recent years, the world market for homemade quilts has expanded dramatically. No longer the preserve of New England homemakers, quilting has become a worldwide industry worth, conservatively, over $300 million.

Huh? Why are you telling me this? Why should I care?

If it turns out that, because of all this hoohah about quilting, the reader of your sales letter could make a fortune investing in quilting technology then good grief, start with that!

And, saving the worst till last, the ultimate cliché with which not to start your sales letter is,

'As a valued client'.

This is at once unoriginal and insulting to your reader, neither approach being likely to secure you further sales. It communicates several (bad) things: that there are clients you don't value; that you are so bored writing to your clients that you resort to clichés; and, given that the next word is invariably 'I', you are unable to write grammatical English.

If a letter is a personal
communication then
it follows you should
use a personal tone
of voice.

Poor use of data

If you have enough data to address a letter to the reader personally, that is, Mr A Maslen, MD, Sunfish Ltd…, make sure you personalise the opening, Dear Mr Maslen.

I have been banking with a certain global bank ever since I started Sunfish in 1996. Yet they still persist in sending me 'customer service' letters that begin, Dear Customer. How difficult can it be to insert a field in the document Dear <salutation> <last name>?

Overlong paragraphs

When confronted with a sales letter, most people begin by assessing it in purely visual terms. They don't read it, they look at it. And they are doing it to form a quick judgement: is this going to be easy to read? If it looks difficult or boring, they won't bother. Why should they – it's only junk mail as far as they're concerned. The single biggest thing you can do to ensure they come to the right conclusion – the conclusion you want them to come to – is by breaking up your text into short paragraphs.

In a letter I would suggest staying under five lines. A one-word, one-line or one-sentence paragraph is fine, regardless of what you or I were taught at school. (I often hear this line of reasoning used by marketeers and copywriters when I suggest doing something that breaks the supposed rules of English. I borrow a line from my father, a lifelong educator, who said, 'But you're not *at* school!')

Impersonal tone of voice

If a letter is a personal communication then it follows you should use a personal tone of voice. That means warm, conversational, friendly, in plain English and, well, personal. Start off by addressing your reader as 'you' and don't let up. Never use the phrase, 'some of you' or address your reader by reference to the group to which they belong, 'this pressure-sensitive diving watch is suitable for divers of all skill levels'.

Once you do, you lose your reader, who senses, rightly, that you aren't really interested in them, just in their money. Cynics would argue that you *are* only interested in their money. But you won't get to *see* it unless you can effect a pretty solid impersonation of someone who finds them the most interesting creature on the planet.

No benefits

I see a lot of sales letters that manage to fill up a couple of sides of A4 without ever giving the reader a reason to buy. Lots of facts about the product, lots of features, but no benefits. You may think it's blindingly obvious why someone should buy your gizmo. But does your reader? Does *every* reader?

So first answer the question, What's in it for me?'. That should ensure you're talking benefits. Then check that your copy actually is talking benefits by asking the question, 'So what?'. If you feel silly asking 'so what?' then you have a genuine benefit. Let's take an example. If you were writing a sales letter for the Acme Stairgate Company, your so-called benefits copy might sound like any of the following:

Our baby gates are manufactured from NASA-grade chrome-moly alloy. *So what*?

This space-age metal is 300% stronger than steel. *So what*?

Even if a child falls directly against it, the gate holds fast, protecting your little one. *Er, OK, how much?*

Too glitzy

Letters should look like letters. In the old days that was a) obvious and b) difficult to deviate from. The technology simply wasn't there to do anything more than lay out the text in a typewriter face and stick your logo at the top. Now the world is your oyster. Photos, screen grabs, a fiesta of fancy typefaces, textured backgrounds... you think of it, your designer can do it. But it's all wrong (or most of it is).

Even though for most people, the only letters these days they receive ARE direct mail, you should still aim to make your letters resemble correspondence. If you do use graphics (and create what

I would call an illustrated letter), restrict images in quantity and placement so they don't interfere with the run of text. Avoid the fancier design techniques – you can incorporate them into your brochure if you really feel they'll help shift merchandise.

Bad typography

Where shall we start? Not with a wholesale description of all the forms bad typography can take. Instead, a little checklist of things to avoid:

- Copy set in too small a point size. Make it easy for your reader to read your copy without reaching for their specs. If you're writing for younger people this is less of a concern, but it still needs to be inviting, which ultra-small type ain't.
- Copy set in a design-y typeface. The best typeface to set direct mail letters in is Courier (or Courier New). After that, Times. After that, any reasonably straight-looking serif typeface. Why? Because they are readable, and in tests have been shown to generate more money. Please avoid making aesthetic judgements about typefaces in promotional literature. Whether it conforms to your personal taste – or brand guidelines – is less important than whether it works.
- Scrunched up leading. Resist the temptation to fit all the copy onto one side of the paper by squishing the leading. Ideally, you want 2–3pt leading, that is, 11pt type on a 13 or 14pt body.
- Multiple typefaces. Two at most please. Maybe a sans serif face for the headlines and a serif for the body copy. One is fine.

No cross-heads

Even in the shortest letter, cross-heads (those headings that run between paragraphs of body copy), help the reader navigate your copy and provide an instant visual cue that says, 'Hey, this is going to be easy to read'.

You can use them to tell the story in outline, although Joe Sugarman, a highly successful US-based mail order copywriter, tested nonsense cross-heads and found even these out-pulled ads with none at all.

No teasers to keep people reading

People *will* read long copy (however you define 'long'). But they need a little help and encouragement. Saying 'But that's not all…' at the end of a paragraph is a simple (if obvious) trick.

Too short

How short is too short? Simple. Your copy is too short if you have left anything out that might have persuaded your reader to buy from you. It doesn't matter how many words you write in a letter, as long as they are relevant to your reader.

No signature

Letters should come from individuals. So ensure yours does and looks like it does. Including a signature – which you can arrange by simply signing a piece of white paper with a black pen then scanning it and saving as a graphic file for your Mac or PC – is the simplest way I know of to achieve this aim.

Signed by a 'team'.

Argh! Please don't end your sales letter, 'Yours sincerely, The Customer Service team'. Or any other team for that matter.

No PS

People read the PS. In fact they read it pretty well immediately after opening the envelope. It sits under the signatory's name, which is one reason. Another is it sits in a little clean area of its own where it's easy to spot. Third is some lingering folk-memory that PSs were added in at the last minute with some interesting news.

What you must include

My feeling is that you should include everything in your sales letter. And by everything I mean every single point you can think of that will help your reader make the decision to buy from you. Here are a few things you should include in a sales letter:

A description of the features of your product or service – translated into benefits. In other words, what your product does for the reader. And make sure you include *all* the reasons why someone might buy from you. You don't know which one will tip the scales in your favour, so it pays to be as comprehensive as possible.

A testimonial or two – or three – from existing customers, that tell the story from a different angle. Make sure your testimonials are genuine and resist the temptation to tidy them up. As long as they are in reasonably correct English, leave them alone.

Copy that raises and resolves any potential objections your prospect might have to buying from you. If your business is new, or the product is, maybe you include endorsements from well-established names in your industry. If it's a high-priced product, you could compare the price to something else the reader is likely to possess, or divide it by 365 and talk about the cost per day. Or compare it to the likely returns that accrue to the reader once they've bought it. If it fits with your industry, product category or business policies, you might think about offering a money-back guarantee. These are used widely in subscriptions marketing within the magazine publishing industry and have been shown to increase response.

A strong call to action that restates the main benefit or benefits, and recaps any offer you are making.

What you can leave out

In my case, I can generally leave out the entire opening paragraph in my first draft. Clients never see these because I delete them in the editing process. It's my way of getting started and dispensing with writer's block, or, more prosaically, not knowing which way to begin out of the dozens I can think of.

If your sales letters begin with sweeping generalisations about your prospect's industry, you can leave this out. People either know it or don't expect to read about it in a sales letter – or both. Either way, it's not as attention-grabbing as many copywriters seem to think.

You can also leave out all but the most cursory descriptions of your company's history and development. People generally don't care. Yes, they want to be sure they are dealing with a reputable organisation, but there are other ways of convincing them than a blow-by-blow account of your company's foundation and growth. Institutional membership logos, awards or satisfaction guarantees will do it for you.

I would also suggest that you leave out, or rather don't introduce in the first place, secondary offers or calls to action. In other words, if you start out with a sales pitch for a pack of craft materials, don't end by offering craft workshops. People are easily confused and won't know whether to order the craft materials or book the workshop. They'll probably end up deferring the decision altogether. On the other hand, selling packs of craft materials *then* writing again to offer seminar places is an excellent idea.

> You can also leave out all but the most cursory descriptions of your company's history and development. People generally don't care.

How to structure it

The main thing you have to do with the structure of a sales letter is get to the point, fast. In this, sales letters aren't so very different from many other channels or marketing media such as emails, web pages or press ads. Here's a suggested approach:

Headline: offering a benefit of some kind, leading with your offer (if you have one), inducing the reader to read by arousing their curiosity – or, best of all, a combination of all three.
Sub-head: following on from the headline and taking a slightly different tack. So if your headline focuses on an appeal to

the reader's self-interest (always a good idea), your subhead might lead with the offer.

Salutation: Dear Ms Jones is best (or Dear Carol if you are very sure of your ground and have the data to back it up). Dear Showjumper is OK. Dear Client or Dear Customer will also do at a pinch, though these days, if you haven't got personal data for your customers, Hello?! Does the word database mean anything to you? I'd advise against Dear Sir/Madam – a surprisingly large number of companies still use this – unless you are hell-bent on sounding like the Fifties never went away.

First paragraph: here is where it all happens. Or doesn't. We've already looked at how *not* to do it. So here's what I recommend instead. You lead with your main benefit. If you are selling chef's knives that never need sharpening, something like this should work:

Dear Mr Brown,

As a keen amateur cook you want the same quality blades you'd find in a top restaurant. But without the high prices. Thanks to a new technology developed in Japan, home to the world's most skilful bladesmiths, this Holy Grail can be yours.

Or you can open with a question. Or three. Asking questions is an excellent method of engaging your reader. If they get as far as your opening paragraph, and it asks them a question, I'd bet the farm they'll start thinking of the answer.

Or you can begin with a story. One of the most famous and best-performing direct mail letters of all time, for the *Wall Street Journal* opened like this: 'On a sunny spring afternoon'. Incidentally, this letter dispensed with a headline and remained unchanged for about 30 years.

However you start, make sure it's not just an exercise in fine writing. You need to get to the point – and the point should be the benefit to your reader. Anything else will quickly become boring. Remember, this is direct mail you're writing here. They didn't ask you to write to them. They weren't expecting you to. And they really don't care whether you do or don't.

Main body: having got to the point and introduced your main benefit, you need to expand on it, prove it and then introduce more benefits. Then you need to introduce more evidence that what you say is true. This leads us on to...

Testimonials: toward the middle or end of your letter you can introduce testimonials. They seem to work best in odd-numbered groups, so go for one or three. Here's how I introduce them:

> Do I sound enthusiastic about the Acme Tulip Bulb Trowel? Of course I do! But then, I'm the guy who invented it. So to give you a more unbiased view, here are a few of our customers talking...

Going over the page: if your letter spans more than one page (and there's absolutely no reason on Earth why it shouldn't) consider very carefully how you're going to get your reader to turn over. Here are a couple of ideas. You can ask them to, politely, by saying, Over please. (Or please turn over, I'm not going to get too bossy here). Or you can do something cleverer, and split your final sentence across the page break. Or you can tease them along a little by saying something like, Five more reasons to try us, overleaf.

The call to action: your close is just that. You have to close the sale. So do it by asking for the order; better yet, command them to order. Say something like:

> Order by 31st January and we'll rush you your free guide to growing competition onions.

The PS: as I said earlier, people tend to read the PS, even if they don't read much else. So use it for a little bit of stealth selling. Recap your main benefit. Restate your call to action. Repeat your offer. Just don't do what an early client of mine once insisted on and say 'PS Please note, price does not include postage and packing, which is charged at £5.95 per book'. I should have been firmer with him but I was new to the game and gave in.

Notes on style and tone of voice

You want to sound conversational, warm and most definitely human.

Most of the channels I discuss in this book call for a pretty similar tone of voice. You want to sound conversational, warm and most definitely human. For sales letters I would say the friendlier the better, without descending into fake mateyness. Keep your style simple and unaffected, use plain English and only use long words when they carry a specific technical meaning or you really can't find a shorter alternative.

Using images

As I've said already, keep images to a minimum in sales letters. The emphasis should be on the copy, particularly since the format is supposed to be emulating 'proper' correspondence. You can use images very creatively in letters, but always be sure that they are adding to the power of the copy and not simply decorating. And be restrained – after all, if you wanted to produce something really colourful and eye-catching, you should be thinking about a brochure or flyer.

Letterhead v special paper

One last thing to consider is what you're going to print your letter on. If it's a small quantity, you may feel tempted to use your standard corporate letterhead. It's OK, but probably designed to reflect all the business needs of your organisation, so it will have lots of space given over to company registration number, directors and all your contact details including your corporate web address.

Far better to have your designer create either a new direct mail-friendly letterhead where the extraneous material is shoved out of the way to make room for your copy or create something brand new specifically for this mailing.

Figure 1 New subscriber acquisition letter for *The Grocer* **magazine**

This direct mail letter follows many of the classic rules, from text emphasis to handwritten copy. But it doesn't have a head-line. The client was happy – the campaign exceeded the targets for new subscriber acquisitions.

Offers.

They used to be the exception. Now they're the rule. So to win you over to The Grocer, I've come up with an unbeatable BOGOF of my own.

Buy one subscription to The Grocer and I'll give you one year's subscription to **thegrocer.co.uk** FREE. That's as plain as I can make it. A saving of £99.50 off the business intelligence package that helps you run a more profitable business.

Data, news, opinion and more

I reckon you're somebody who doesn't want to stand still. Somebody who wants to see their business thrive, whatever the economic conditions. Somebody who wants to make progress in our industry. That makes you pretty smart. We can make you smarter still.

Want to know how the big five are pricing the most popular grocery items? Turn to **thegrocer33**. Need to know who's moving where? **movers&shakers** tells you. Interested in who's launching which new products in your sector? It couldn't be easier thanks to **food&drinknews**.

And if you like to know who's getting their feathers ruffled, we've enough outspoken **comment&opinion** to keep so-called policymakers, complacent management and industry 'experts' on the back foot.

Get the insider's viewpoint

In fact, with The Grocer on your team, you're always in the loop. You're among the first to know of new trends. New market entrants. New products. New consumer trends. New UK or European laws that could affect you or your company.

Now, you're the one ahead of the trend. You're the one able to make the right buying decisions. You're the one coming up with the products UK consumers will hand over their hard-earned cash for. Even in the credit crunch. Why?

Because you have the insider's grasp of what makes our industry tick. From Fairtrade to price wars, new

Seven great reasons to subscribe

CHAPTER 3
CASE STUDY

HOW I HELPED
BUSINESSES
EXPLAIN WHAT
THEY DO: A
SUNFISH CASE
STUDY

Introduction

Case studies are an excellent way of showing potential clients just how good you are at whatever it is you do.

A case study is simply a story about how you solved some problem for one of your clients or customers. It can be copy-only or you can include images and graphics.

Case studies have their origins in business schools, where they are used to teach the future masters of the universe about real world business problems and, hopefully, how to solve them. Given how many monumental cock-ups are committed by teams of management consultants, it seems the jury's out on whether this teaching method's any good. However…

Case studies are an excellent way of showing potential clients just how good you are at whatever it is you do. They tell stories, which is a good thing, and they tell the truth, which is an even better thing. By writing a case study you are almost forced to see the world from your client's perspective. You can't get away with writing reams of copy that simply describes your product or service and its features. Instead, you have to explain, and show, how users of your product benefit. Since this is what any potential client is interested in anyway, it seems like a fine place to start.

There's no set length for a case study either. It all depends on the complexity of the problem – or challenge – that you are talking about. A case study can be ultra-short:

> Bill Evans was a disaster at the dating game until, with our help, he mastered the art of conversation. Thanks to our self-study DVDs and website Bill is now happily married with three beautiful children. 'I couldn't have done it without *Talk Yourself Married*,' says Bill.

Or it can run for several hundred, or thousand, words. Just be sure you are always making relevant points and further convincing your reader of the wisdom of doing business with you.

Strengths

The case study's main strength is that it appears to be less about sales and more about education, or information. Its purpose is to sell, but not directly. It serves to warm up your prospect, to overcome their objections and to answer some of their initial questions about what you do and whether it's any good. Done properly it includes viewpoints other than that of the writer so it provides impartial testimony.

People are less sceptical when they read a case study. It is serious, authoritative and packed with facts. When you write a case study, the bulk of the work is in the research and planning stages. Actually drafting the copy shouldn't take very much time at all, because you are really concentrating on an almost journalistic approach – telling it like it is – or was, without the need to dress it up.

Weaknesses

Because you generally need a fair amount of space to write a good case study the implication is that your prospect will need a fair amount of time to read it. Time, as we know, is in diminishing supply these days – always has been, really. So plonking a 2,000-word case study in front of a busy potential client might be more off-putting than enticing.

The key, as with any longer copy, is to ensure it's relevant to your reader. Design can play a strong role too in breaking up your copy and presenting it in an attractive, highly navigable format that leads the reader gently through the whole thing.

And because it's only what you would call sales support, it is never going to make the sale on its own, unlike an ad, sales letter or email. So it will have to be accompanied by other materials, maybe as part of a sales kit or bigger mailing.

What you can use it for

Case studies are particularly suited to more sophisticated products and especially services. If you are selling bird feeders, bicycles or bananas, you probably won't need a case study. If, on the other hand, you are writing copy to promote any of the following, we're in business:

- Marketing agency
- Management consultancy
- IT provider
- Law firm
- Property development services
- Media or advertising
- PR consultant
- Executive coaching
- Facilities management
- Contract publishing
- Industrial plant manufacture
- Scientific services for industry
- Management training

What you are trying to do is *prove* to your prospect that all the things you say about yourself in your marketing campaign (of which the case study is itself a part) are *true*. That, yes, were they to take you up on your offer, they too would benefit in all the ways the subject of your case study did.

What goes wrong

Insufficient research

The secret of a really good case study is research. Imagine you are a journalist writing an article on the same subject. You wouldn't just sit down and make it up (well you might but you're not that sort of journalist). You'd do your background reading, you'd interview the key people involved and you'd find out everything you needed to about the process or product being demonstrated in the case study. The result would be a very good article – or case study.

Without enough research you are forced back into generalities. You can only talk about your client 'making significant savings' rather than 'making savings of £75,000 a year on recruitment and training.' Or 'after several months of work' rather than 'after a two and a half month process involving focus groups, concept development and advertising pre-testing'.

What's worse, your reader can spot your fluffy evasions a mile off. You headed this piece of copywriting with the words 'case study' and that raises certain expectations – quite high expectations – in your reader's mind. The devil is in the detail they say, and without enough research you won't be able to describe what happened – tell the story, in other words – in enough detail to make it believable.

Too short

A parallel concern to the problem of poor research is that your case study is too short. I said in the introduction to this section that case studies can be ultra short – but at that point they are really more like turbocharged testimonials. In truth, your reader, if they decide to read your case study at all, wants some meat they can get their teeth into. Want an arbitrary word count? I'd say no fewer than 300. That's only around half a page of A4 and shouldn't be unduly taxing if you've done your research.

Too long

Remember, this is not a doctoral thesis or academic case study, it's a piece of marketing communications. That means you want something your reader can read through and digest in one sitting, and I don't mean a 17-course banquet type of sitting either. Something more like a quick lunch. If you are printing your case study, you should have something that will fill, comfortably, a four-page A4 brochure without resorting to tiny type or no pictures to squeeze it all in.

A case study gives you a chance to let your clients do the selling for you.

No client viewpoint

What brings a case study alive is the client's perspective. Leave it out and all you have is an extended boast dressed up in worthier clothes than a pure sales pitch. Just as with a testimonial on its own, a case study gives you a chance to let your clients do the selling for you. They should be providing unbiased opinions of your service that let others know just how good you are.

No coherent storyline

Any good story needs a beginning, a middle and an end. It should also have believable characters and a narrative that explains how the hero overcame a challenge. This classic story structure and ingredients list is why case studies work so well. So make sure you follow the rules of storytelling.

Dotting around, using too many parallel narrative devices such as bullet points, callouts, panels and flowcharts will confuse rather than engage your reader. It's best to start with a simple statement of the problem facing your client and work forwards from there.

No images

Think of a case study as akin to a children's illustrated story rather than a novel. In other words, you need pictures. Even if the picture in question is just a photo of your client looking happy with a quote from them underneath. Without any graphics at all, you are relying on your reader's willingness to sit down and read pure copy. They might do that with a sales letter, where the personal tone of voice is more engaging, but case studies are necessarily less conversational in tone and for that reason, more of a struggle. A few well chosen images lift the case study and provide some visual relief from the text.

No call to action

Although a case study is not a direct sales piece, you'd be a fool to spend all that time and money producing one without making it work a little harder for its corn. So it's a mistake to leave out a call to action. Just including your contact details isn't enough. Instead, you need a soft call to action that invites your prospect to contact you for more information, a free trial, a consultation, more background research from the case study or even another case study.

What you must include

As you've probably figured out by now, you have to include as much detail as possible. The best and most persuasive sort of detail is hard figures that quantify any benefits the client derived by using your company, product or service. I'd also suggest the following:

- A profile of the client. This should include a brief mention of their organisation name, the client contact's name and job title, their industry and any other details that flesh them out for your reader. We hope that the reader will identify with the client in the case study, so give them enough material to make the connection.
- A timeline of some sort, so the reader can see how the project or process worked over time and as a sequence.
- A detailed description of the problem or challenge facing the client and that led them to come to you for help.
- Background on your organisation and what particular skills, experience, products, technologies or processes you could call on to help your client.
- Details of what exactly you did.
- How the project turned out. Obviously this is going to be a positive outcome, but you can paint a picture so the reader sees how your input led to the outcome.
- Glowing remarks from the client, either couched as picture captions, pull quotes or interview-style quotations in the body copy,

What you can leave out

You can leave out anything that will be too technical for the average reader of the case study to understand. Also, despite my pleading for detail, be selective. Your aim is to provide just enough detail for the story to be believable. You are not writing a manual that will enable your reader to replicate your results on their own.

I'd also suggest omitting long slabs of copy describing your organisation. The way you tend to use case studies means the reader will already have found you and accessed information about your organisation. The stage they are at when they request, download or read a case study is beyond the ground-level research of finding out who you are and reading the About Us page on your website.

And avoid the temptation to include any obviously salesy copy. This is not the place to start listing benefits or '10 reasons to work with us'. Keep it clean and neutral in tone for maximum effect.

How to structure it

Headline: your main headline is like the title of your story. It doesn't necessarily need to promise a benefit like an ad headline or sales letter, though it can. What you do need to is encapsulate the challenge. You might write something like this:

> Creating a more effective public consultation system for Northminster City Council

Sub- or super-head: under or over your main headline you need to make it clear to the reader that what they are reading is a case study. This is one of the rare occasions where you do actually want to merely label a piece of marketing collateral. So, you have a short line that reads:

> A Sunfish Ltd case study

Introductory paragraph: here's where you fall back on the old journalistic technique of answering the questions who, what, where, when and why? In your opening paragraph, give your reader the whole story in outline. Not the detail, just the bare bones. You're going to expand on them later. It's what magazine editors call a standfirst: the shortest paragraph that sits between the head-line and the body of the article and draws the reader into the text.

First section: describe the challenge or problem the client was facing. It's best to couch it in terms that suggests there was some benefit that was just out of reach if only they could surmount the obstacle in the way. This sets you up to go on to describe how you arrived on the scene and put things right.

This is also the place where you can introduce the main character: your client. They realised what was needed was outside help and you can reveal how they realised that outside help was you or your organisation. Perhaps they'd read about your work with another business in their industry. Maybe they did some web research. However you do it, show your reader how you came to be selected. The more due diligence the client did before picking you to help them, the wiser a choice it seems for your reader to skip that stage and come directly to you.

Second section: having explained the set-up and the route the client took to finding you, you can outline the benefits they could expect to enjoy from working with you. Are you fast? Do you have more experience in this area than anyone else? Have you won awards? Do your clients typically go on to experience industry-leading levels of staff retention or profitability or engineering success? Whatever the outcome, you can point to it here.

Third section: now you need to explain exactly what happened. Describe the process, but try to keep it interesting. That means introducing more people, telling your reader what happened in engaging language, using dates, describing any (minor) setbacks and how you overcame them. Think about your favourite writers of fiction and how they keep you reading. Cliff-hangers, unexpected developments, changes of pace: these are all devices you can import into your copywriting. You can even introduce dialogue by quoting the main players on both sides in turn. This allows you to vary the style and register of your copy and gives your reader a break from the narrative.

Fourth section: you've described the process and the story is nearing completion. Tell your reader what happened in the end. When everything that needed to be done was done, did the client get the desired benefits you outlined in section two? How much exactly? Where exactly? In which parts of the business or market? Provide figures if you can or some other way of putting a value on your contribution. Another quote from the satisfied client would work well here.

Fifth section: it's not over till it's over, and you can suggest that there's still more to come. Perhaps you are continuing to work with the client in other areas of the business. Or the project expanded to include new activities. This sows an important seed in your reader's mind that working with you is about long-term relationships, which will be more profitable for you. A simple heading that works here is 'Next steps'.

Final section: this is where you make your play for their business. The call to action in other words. Remember to keep it friendly and non-salesy. Provide all your contact details and, if possible, create some sort of incentive to encourage the reader to contact you. A further case study, a no-obligation business health-check or a free 30-minute consultation could all work, if you are prepared to resource them.

You could also include brief details of your organisation especially if you can pull out the aspects of your service that match the likely needs of the reader.

Notes on style and tone of voice

For a case study, you should adopt a fairly serious style and tone of voice. You want to come across as professional, experienced, knowledgeable and authoritative rather than warm and fuzzy. This is all about positioning yourself as the experts – the go-to guys – rather than as the reader's new best friend. (That will come later.)

You demonstrate that you care about your customers by fleshing out the case study with details of your commitment to solving their problems, rather than by snuggling up to the reader. Aim for a style you'd expect to see in a broadsheet newspaper or, perhaps, *The Economist*. Just remember that this particular magazine will cheerfully call a spade a spade and not a horticultural cavity excavation facilitator.

You write case studies in the past tense. This is, after all, a story of something that's already happened. A sentence to introduce the problem might read like this:

> When Jarndyce & Jarndyce discovered their client records system couldn't cope with legal requirements in the Far East, they knew they had to address the problem fast. Their newly launched Hong Kong practice was on the brink of winning five major corporate deals that would flounder if they fell foul of the regulators.

And to avoid your case study sounding too much like an academic paper or sludgy corporate record, write in the active voice as far as you can. Like this:

> Harry Mills, head of chambers in Hong Kong, decided to contact Sunfish because he'd read of our success with another law firm in Singapore.

Rather than this:

> Sunfish was contacted by Harry Mills, head of chambers in Hong Kong, after it had been discovered that another law firm in Singapore had been helped by us.

Using images

One thing to remember here – try to avoid library images. Case studies are records of what actually happened so you should have at least one photograph that illustrates the story. The moment people see a stock shot the not-so-subtle subtext is, *this is not true*.

Figure 2 Case study on a partnership between the British Standards Institution and the Federation Against Software Theft (FAST)

If you are quoting personnel from your client, get their mugshots. Or arrange for them to have one taken. Even a shot of their premises is better than nothing. Caption all your images and, if they are photos of your client's team, use a quote as the caption.

You may want to illustrate the process with a flowchart, timeline or other graphic. That's fine as long as they don't interfere with the flow of copy or dominate it to the extent that it's easier just to look at the pictures. Alone they won't tell the story in sufficient depth to convince the reader to hire you.

When you're writing a case study, you can structure it like an article, with a headline, standfirst, cross heads, quotes and photographs.

Remember to include a call to action and focus on how you solved the client's problem.

Building credibility, increasing take-up of the internal standard

FAST Corporate Services already had an internal standard for software management. It wanted to raise the profile of the standard amongst its members and bring in additional authority to enhance its credibility. There was only one solution to meet these needs: working with BSI to produce a Private Standard.

FAST – the Federation Against Software Theft – exists to protect software publishers' rights in their intellectual property. At its simplest, that means stopping people making or distributing illegal copies of popular software. The organization was set up in 1984 as an offshoot of the British Computer Society's copyright committee. By 1991 it had 200 publishers as members, and in the following year it opened its doors to corporate members. These, after all, were the people using the software.

FAST Corporate Services provides an education programme for its 2,700 corporate members that focuses on the effective management of software assets. Compliance with the Copyright, Designs and Patents Act 1988 is a major part of its remit.

The keystone of FAST Corporate Services' offering to its members is the FAST audit and certification programme. Audit Certification is the mark of excellence in software management. The staged corporate membership programme helps organizations ...

- **identify** and eliminate risks relating to IT management
- **expose** illegal software
- **set up** purchasing and installation procedures
- **educate** staff
- **maximize** the ROI in their IT assets.

It enables them to demonstrate that they are fully compliant with the law. Originally, it was underpinned by an internal standard – the FAST Standard.

FAST CORPORATE PROGRAMME

The FAST Standard for Software Compliance (FSSC 1:2004) is a private standard developed in collaboration with BSI.

The challenge: add value, raise awareness

The FAST Standard is a wide-ranging document. It includes everything from software procurement policies, such as the documenting and cataloguing of invoices and licences, to practical ways of ensuring buy-in from all relevant members of staff.

It is complemented by the FAST programme stages, which include bronze, silver, gold and platinum, and awards for FAST-approved software managers and auditors.

How could FAST encourage even greater take-up of the standard? How could they enhance the value of the standard for qualifying companies?

Collaborating with BSI – a four-point value proposition

By working with BSI Professional Services, FAST aimed to gain in four key areas:

- Increased credibility of the FAST Standard
- Improved awareness among the membership
- Increase in membership and certification
- Increase in revenue

"Our goal is to promote compliance through education and to see more companies compliant with copyright legislation."

Chris Minchin
Membership Manager
FAST Corporate Services

The FAST internal review committee

Geoff Webster,
CEO

Peter Kay,
Director of Services

Chris Minchin,
Membership Manager

plus members of the
FAST Corporate Services
and FAST Consultancy
Services teams

The solution: leverage the BSI brand and knowledge

The answer lay in partnering with a recognizable brand. A brand known worldwide for the quality and rigour of its standards. The BSI brand. Initially, discussions focused on turning the FAST Standard into a full British Standard. However, two challenges immediately presented themselves.

First, the development process would take too long. Second, FAST Corporate Services had devoted considerable resources and effort to creating their standard. It represented a valuable piece of intellectual property in its own right. They wanted to retain ownership and control, so that they could continue to benefit commercially from implementation, education and training around the standard.

Fitting the bill: a Private Standard proved the ideal solution

With BSI's guidance, the favoured choice emerged as the Private Standard. Private Standards are founded on the rigorous BSI processes of standards development, but without the need for such extensive consultation, consensus or public availability. However, they still represent a significant leap in quality and editorial rigour compared with even the best-written internal documents.

Chris Minchin, Membership Manager for FAST Corporate Services, explains: "The benefits of a full British Standard are clear, but we needed to retain a strong hold on the standard. We are a commercial organization whose entire reason for existing revolves around protecting intellectual property rights."

"We needed a middle way between a full British Standard and a wholly internal document: the Private Standard offered us just that position."

Even though FAST opted for a Private Standard, they were still able to take advantage of BSI's extensive community of experts within the IT sector.

The process
Drafting

After discussions over the extent and content of the new Private Standard, the project went live. The first step was for Chris Minchin to write the first draft using the FAST Standard as the starting point. Chris comments: "We already had a very tight document but we knew we could really raise the bar by involving BSI. They would also add their knowledge and expertise in drafting standards."

Once the first draft was complete, it passed to a BSI Project Manager whose job was to take Chris's draft and ensure it met BSI's stringent criteria for the format and language appropriate to Private Standards.

The Project Manager was able to draw on BSI's strong and established position within the international IT sector. BSI has facilitated the development of, and published, a wide range of technical and management standards including:

- BS 7799 – Information Security Management
- BS 15000 – IT Service Management
- BS 15489 – Information and Records Management

It also provides guidance and training to IT standards, legislation and regulation such as the Data Protection and Freedom of Information Acts, Legal Admissibility and Privacy.

Consultation

The consultation phase came next. Once the first draft had been shaped into the required format for a Private Standard it passed to an internal FAST committee for comments and feedback. BSI was able to advise on every detail of the consultation process, including best practice in securing and incorporating feedback from members.

continued →

CHAPTER 4
PRESS
RELEASE

**'BORING PRESS
RELEASES GET
THROWN IN
BIN' SAYS
COPYWRITER**

Introduction

PR really is free advertising.

PR really is free advertising. Without the taint of commercialism. But you do have to work a little harder. Journalists are under no obligation to print what you send them, unlike their more accommodating colleagues in the advertising department. So give them something usable, write it well, and sprinkle a few quotes around.

A press (or media or news) release is a standardised way of announcing some news to the media. There is fairly broad agreement on format, style and structure between the media outlets on the receiving end and the PR companies and companies doing their own PR on the other. We'll cover all that in this chapter.

You have to remember that precisely because it is a press release, and not an ad or sales piece, you must avoid selling. This might sound odd coming from a copywriter but believe me, the fastest route into the journalist's Deleted Items folder is to come over all super-smashing-great.

You have to imagine that you are the journalist writing the article. You wouldn't hock your professional ethics to a company you'd never heard of, regurgitating a thinly-disguised sales pitch as a news article. Instead you'd want to write something that would be of genuine interest to your readers. If, in passing, you mentioned the name and specialism of the company behind the story, well, that's because leaving it out would mean not telling the full story.

The key to a good press release lies in the subject matter – and how you present it. Remember that journalists are looking for something that they think will interest their readers. They want something that will fit the overall style and tone of their paper/magazine/programme/website.

Strengths

From an operational standpoint, the best thing about press releases is that they cost relatively little. If you're writing them in-house you spend about as much time, maybe a little less, as you would on an ad or sales letter. If you are commissioning an external copywriter, you'd similarly pay around about the same amount as for a short ad or web page. If you have a PR agency, well, you may never discover how much you're paying, but then you wouldn't be reading this unless you were planning to change.

From a marketing standpoint, if you get your press release into the media you have independent endorsement of your company and its products and services. It's not an ad, so the reader isn't suspicious. And because it's editorial there's a much higher chance they'll read it. You can also then use the cutting itself in publicity campaigns (subject to getting copyright clearance of course) and place it in your reception area in a folder titled 'XYZ Company, Media Coverage'.

You should also get some measurable results, over and above any notional 'awareness'. When I was running an in-house PR operation, we used to ask every caller, 'what prompted you to call us today?' and fill in the answer on our call log. When I consolidated the results I discovered that 16% of inbound calls were prompted by media coverage. We never made the final step and tracked sales back to media coverage but it's a fair bet there would have been hundreds of thousands of pounds' worth of business directly attributable to our original press releases.

Weaknesses

The great weakness of press releases is the mirror image of their great strength: because you're placing yourself in the hands of a journalist, you can't control what happens. You can spend time, effort and money planning, writing and distributing thousands of the damn things only to find you get no coverage. If your soft news happens to coincide with a war – or even a celebrity staggering drunk out of a club – there's a chance your story will get spiked. However, if you go about it in the right way, you *will* get coverage: just don't regard it as a straight-line graph between number of releases issued and amount of column inches.

A further weakness of press releases is that because they are supposed to be objective – news, in fact – you can't blow your own trumpet. You must be discreet. But that's like accusing rowing boats of being slower than speedboats, or elephants of lacking agility.

What you can use it for

A press release is, in essence, an announcement. An announcement of news, in fact. But the definition of news gets a bit blurry. Here are a few ideas for news stories you could promote to the media with a press release (in no particular order):

- New product
- New service
- Research or survey results
- A new hire, especially a senior position
- New premises
- An event you are holding
- Charity involvement
- Environmental developments
- Community projects
- Sports or other sponsorship
- Opening a new office (locally, regionally, nationally or internationally)
- Books or articles published by staff members
- Speeches given by staff members
- Advice on hobbies (for business-to-consumer 'b2c' companies)
- Advice on business best practice (for business-to-business 'b2b' companies)

What goes wrong

No relevance to the target media's audience

A journalist will only use your press release if it meets the following condition:

It must be relevant to their audience.

Local news stories about how you rescued a dilapidated watermill and turned it into B1 industrial space will not interest the editors of national newspapers or international business magazines.

Stories about how you successfully applied for and were awarded ISO 9001 status are unlikely to make it into the pages of *Practical Woodworker*. In other words, think about your reader. You don't have to create a separate press release for every single media outlet on your list, but it makes sense to figure out who will be interested in your story then either target them specifically or create a few versions with a different flavour or hook for the broad sections of the media that you are contacting.

Bad subject line

Although you can send out press releases by post or even fax, most these days will go out by email. Either directly from your company or via a distribution service. That means you'll need a subject line. And the tip here is don't start your subject line: PRESS RELEASE. Journalists are used to getting press releases in their inbox so they don't need telling. It's a bit like writing JUNK MAIL on the outer envelope of your mailshot.

Bad headline

Assuming the hard-pressed hack opens your email, the first thing they'll read is your headline. As long as you remember you are trying to gain their attention you should be fine. But avoid headlines like this:

The XYZ Corporation is delighted to announce that it has relaunched its website

Like we care!

Slow start

Maybe your headline is a cracker and it's stopped the journalist in their tracks. So they go on to the opening paragraph. This is where you dive straight in and tell the story in outline. Not where you light your pipe, lean back in your armchair and begin, 'Well, my boy, let me tell you how your grandfather started this wonderful business back when the old King was on the throne'.

Beyond your company name, and maybe the briefest of explanations of your line of business, leave your corporate profile until the end. If there's something newsworthy in your release (and if there isn't, why are you sending one out?) get it out there immediately.

Boring/no news

What journalists want is a story. A news story. If you don't have any news, they won't use your press release. In fact (and worse) they will mentally add a sticker on your card in their Rolodex, little black book, or Outlook addresses folder, saying '*timewaster*'.

You may be very excited about launching your best-selling product in a new colour or pack size, but that doesn't make it news. The deal is, you get free advertising in return for doing some work on creating a news story that will save the journalist some time. And remember, it has to be interesting to their readers, as well as to them personally. So think about the ultimate reader as well as the journalist, whom you can think of as a professional filter.

Naked sales pitch

Journalists aren't stupid (though according to some of my journalist friends, they are lazy). If you send an ad reformatted as a press release they will delete it as fast as they are able. Clues abound in press releases like this, usually in the form of overblown language where a new product is always 'revolutionary' or 'unique' and a new technology always 'groundbreaking' or, still, 'cutting edge'. Any claim made without supporting evidence will be similarly treated. 'Hugely popular' hair regrowth products better have some statistics to back up their best mate status among the nation's balding men.

Bad use of English

You are writing for a primary audience of writers. So be especially careful not to commit any errors of grammar, punctuation, spelling or style. Journalists have a never-ending stream of press releases to pick through and will cheerfully discard any that flag the author's lack of attention to detail.

I'd include, in this section, using jargon. Unless there's a specifically technical meaning to a word that means it is the only one that will do, avoid all industry or business jargon. You will not impress journalists by talking about any of the following:

- Low-hanging fruit
- Getting our (or anyone else's) ducks in a row
- Singing from the same hymn-sheet
- Strategic anything
- Going forward
- Communications modalities
- Paradigms (especially if in the process of being shifted)

What you must include

Before you put pen to paper (quaint expression, I know, but I like it), write a plan. What is the big story? Is there a secondary story? How and why will this be of interest to your target audience? Seems obvious, but local papers like a local angle, national papers like a broader angle that appeals to everyone, and specialist media like something that is more focused.

The classic PR method is to answer 'Who? What? Where? When? Why? And How?' in your opening paragraph. This is

> You are writing for a primary audience of writers. So be especially careful not to commit any errors of grammar, punctuation, spelling or style.

certainly a great way to begin but remember also to inject at least a small spark – something that will catch the journalist's imagination and/or curiosity.

Apart from the story itself, there are a few elements that are mandatory for every press release:

The words Press release
Release or embargo date
Either Ends at the end of the story, or (more common in the US) three centred #s, like this:

A line offering contact details for the person who can provide further information.
A *brief* profile of your organisation, which you can introduce with the words, 'Notes for editors'
Details of any photo opportunity.

What you can leave out

Starting from the premise that a press release is a news story you write that you hope the journalist will use, you should leave out anything that is irrelevant to the story. So, great swathes of boiler-plate outlining the history and development of your organisation. *Cut.* Puff, hype and other varieties of over-inflated sales claims. *Cut.* Flowery adjectives, waffle and repetition. *Cut!*

If you feel the need to see all this stuff in print (or on screen) you know you have an alternative – pay for it.

How to structure it

First, at the top of the page, write Press release. Or News release. This is one of a number of standards that you have to adhere to. It tells the journalist at a glance what they're looking at and how, ideally, they should respond to it.

Then the date. There are two formats here:

30 November 2009
For immediate release

Embargoed until:
00:01 30 November 2009

The first format means journalists can use the release as soon as they get it. The second means they have to wait until the date and time specified. Generally, you would only use embargoes if there's some other timed event or announcement that the release must not pre-empt. Having said that, you can stretch the point a little. When writing press releases for the research company I used to work for, we'd always embargo press releases until some nominal publication date to create a sense of topicality even if the report in question had already been sent to clients.

Then your headline. Newspapers and magazines have highly paid people writing the headlines that will actually appear in print. Your headline has an audience of one: the journalist. Its job is to grab their attention (just like an ad headline) and get them to open your press release – because you can use your headline as the subject line if you're distributing via email. Unlike ad headlines, the press release headline should encapsulate the story rather than promise benefits or appeal to the reader's self interest. (In a sense the whole point of press releases is that they appeal to the journalist's desire to get their work done quicker and with less effort.)

Try to come up with a headline that will arrest the journo's instinct to lob your carefully crafted missive into the trash (whether literally or virtually). News is good, but ask yourself whether the news you want to get talked about is news from their point of view. Your new product might have the sales team and half the Board dancing naked in the streets with joy unconfined, but will it have that effect on a bunch of cynical hacks? Here are a few things I have found to work well:

- Giving main survey findings, e.g. 'Teens say no to careers in business'
- Promising a list, e.g. 'Sunfish points the finger at top seven copywriting sins'
- Using a cliché, e.g. 'Sunfish names and shames brand pirates'
- Using sex, e.g. 'Lie back and think of England, says new report'
- Using gender, e.g. 'Women now better copywriters than men, says Sunfish'
- Using geography, e.g. 'No good copywriters outside London, says report'
- Using wordplay, e.g. 'Black day for white goods, says research firm'
- Using statistics, e.g. 'One in four copywriters now vegetarian, says Sunfish'
- Being controversial, e.g. 'Copywriting 'irrelevant to selling' claims guru'

If you are working with local media, you may find you have an easier ride, and a headline that simply tells the story works equally well. In which case, keep it short and to the point and aim for the style you see in your local paper.

XYZ Company opens new office in Anytown

Is better than

The directors and staff of XYZ Company are delighted with their new offices in Anytown

You can also use a sub-head where you flesh out the story in more detail. You are drawing the journalist further into your story without forcing them to read the body copy.

First paragraph. This is critical. As I said earlier, you have to give the news story, quickly, and explain who's doing what, why, where, when and how. Avoid hype or gushy prose in favour of a straight journalistic (there's that word again) telling of the facts. This is all you want – or should want. You can dress it up however you like on your website or in your advertising, but for the press release stick to what you can prove.

Second paragraph. Introduce supporting evidence and go into more detail on the main story. Just remember to keep focused on what the reader wants to read, not what you want to say. You may have all sorts of 'messages' you are keen to get across to potential customers but journalists are not interested in helping you sell more widgets.

Third paragraph. Time for a quote. Quotes are an excellent way to enliven press releases. Journalists like to be able to give the impression that they have researched a story before writing it. Provide them with a few quotes and you make their lives easier: a service for which they will thank you. Here's the classic format:

'Writing press releases opened my eyes to a whole new sphere of linguistic contortions,' said Andy Maslen, Managing Director of Sunfish. 'Knowing what journalists wanted made it far easier to get started, too,' he added.

Some people like to put their quotes in the present tense (says, continues). This is fine – really more a matter of taste than anything else. Just be consistent. Quotes can come from customers, business partners, affiliates, sales agents, members of staff, your CEO, it doesn't really matter as long as they are relevant to the story. If the quote comes from outside your company, make sure you have the person's permission to quote them in your press release (as a courtesy if nothing else).

Fourth/final paragraph. Conclude with a few sentences that explain the link back to your company and its particular skills/experience. Don't go overboard here, keep it factual and to the point.

You end with 'Ends' or three ###s .

Notes for editors and contact details. Give the contact details (landline, mobile, email, postal address) for the person who will field any media enquiries. And a brief profile of your company.

You can stick in a slightly self-glorifying line or two here. Sometimes journalists are short of space and will cut and paste this information at the end of the story. If they do, you can cheerfully refer to your company as 'the leading provider of widget solutions': *Widgets Monthly'* in other publicity materials.

Notes on style and tone of voice

You should write press releases in the third person. Like this:

> XYZ Company today announces it will manufacture all its products using carbon-neutral technology.

Not in the first person like this:

> AT XYZ Company, we are pleased to announce…

Your style should be concise, short and free of flowery language, hype and jargon.

Your style should be concise, short and free of flowery language, hype and jargon as already noted. Keep sentence length down – 10-16 words on average is great. Remember, you don't want the journalist running out of enthusiasm for reading because if they do, it'll never see the light of day.

Use the active voice. Like this:

> XYZ Company is now giving its customers the option of a carry-away service on its grand pianos.

Not the passive, like this:

> Customers of XYZ Company are now being given the option of a carry-away service on its grand pianos.

The tone of voice should be dispassionate, neutral: in a word, journalistic. Avoid breathless phrases like, 'In an exciting new development…' or 'Known for its revolutionary new technologies…'

In terms of length, the shorter the better. If you can say what you have to say in one page or screen rather than two, do it. You get no points for padding. If your release is interesting but the journalist wants more, they have your contact details to get in touch. Having said that, I used to send out six or seven-page press releases and get them picked up by the *Financial Times* and other equally stringent media outlets. The easy answer to the 'how long' question is, 'As long as it needs to be. But no longer.' Like every other form of copywriting.

Using images

You can attach images to a press release. In the old days, that meant enclosing glossy prints with the details sticky-taped to the back. Nowadays you're more likely to be attaching hi-res JPEG files to an email. Or you could include a couple of lines in the release itself about a photo-opportunity where journalists can come along to take their own pictures.

The rule is, provide something interesting, relevant, distinctive and preferably not a cliché – so no grinning executives in front of new premises then.

Three points to bear in mind:

a) The image must be of sufficient quality. For digital that means high-resolution – your digital camera is fine; your mobile phone isn't.
b) Copyright – you must own it or have a licence to use it.
c) Caption – always supply one so the journalist knows what the photo is showing.

media *release*

Embargo: No publication or broadcast before:

00:01am on Wednesday 25 March, 2009

Record-breaking half a million people take part in RSPB's 30th Big Garden Birdwatch
Tit makes tail-end of top ten

More than 552,000 people took part in this year's Big Garden Birdwatch, counting over 8.5 million birds. 73 species were recorded in 279,000 gardens across the UK over the weekend of 24 and 25 January.

And the long-tailed tit has flown into the top ten for the first time in the survey's 30-year history. Numbers of this highly sociable species nearly doubled compared to last year (1).

The increase is being linked to the mild winters leading up to 2009. Small, insect eating birds like long tailed tits are particularly susceptible to the cold as the food they rely on is hard to come by in frosts and snow so milder conditions have contributed to a higher survival rate.

Over the last ten years the long-tailed tit has also adapted to feeding on seeds and peanuts at bird tables and from hanging feeders. This behaviour has spread as they've learnt from each other that tables and feeders offer a wide variety of food .

Figure 3 Press release for the Royal Society for the Protection of Birds' 30th Big Garden Birdwatch

'We wanted to convey the passion and personality of the RSPB and the people who work for it. Given that most press release copy has to be straight narrative, getting the quote right is the key way to achieve this. Plain, conversational English is the order of the day.

'It was given full-page treatments in the *Times, Independent* and *Guardian* and was also well featured in the *Telegraph, Sun* and *Mirror*. The *Today* programme covered it live in a prime 07.40 slot and on news bulletins. It was on Radio 2 and 3 and the *Guardian* podcast.'

Paul Lewis, Head of Public Relations, RSPB

CHAPTER 5
PRODUCT
BROCHURE

**INTRODUCING
THE NEW WAY
TO WRITE
PROMOTIONAL
COPY**

Introduction

Brochure, leaflet, flyer, cut sheet, sales piece: whatever you call it, I'm talking about the sheet of paper (or, increasingly, the PDF) that gives your prospective customer the information they need to buy what you're selling. 'I thought that was the sales letter!' someone yells from the back. 'Or the ad!' calls another. It can be. Though these often focus more on the benefits rather than the features. The definitions can get a bit hazy. If you have a 32-page saddle-stitched (stapled) sales letter complete with illustrations and an order form, who's to say that's not a brochure?

Different industries have different terms for the brochures they create. One woman's brochure is another woman's leaflet. There's no technical definition of what makes a brochure different to a leaflet. I'd only venture to say a leaflet is skimpier, in terms of both weight of paper and amount, and often format. A four-page A5 piece, printed on 115 gsm stock, I would call a leaflet. A 12-page A4 piece, printed on 250 gsm stock, I would call a brochure.

Here's what I think makes a brochure a brochure, and not some other kind of marketing piece.

It's impersonal. Or, immediate correction, it used to be. But now, with the advances in digital printing and data integration, you can have personalised brochures. At any rate, the copy feels less personal.

It's often very 'designer'-looking. Photography, graphics, print rather than typewriter typefaces, lots of white space, typography and layout, format, gloss paper, spot varnish and all sorts of other graphic design or printing techniques.

It has a lower proportion of copy to images. In a letter, 75:25 copy to images might feel like the maximum; in a brochure it could easily be 10:90.

Overall, from a copywriter's perspective, the main difference is that brochures tend, for the same amount of paper, to have less copy than letters. You aren't trying to pack it in to make the sale: you know that there's a sales person (either flesh and blood or in letter form) to close the deal. That means, if you're a freelance, you may charge less than you would for a letter of the same format: it depends if you charge by the word or not.

Strengths

Because they *are* brochures, readers expect them to be a bit flash and not to speak to them directly. This gives you some leeway in how you present the information you want to convey. They are great for presenting product details in a way that a stand-alone letter can struggle with. If you want a panel with a list of 20 bullet points listing technical features of your carbon-fibre fishing rod go ahead!

You also have unlimited space (or as much space as you're prepared to pay for) to show product photographs. The higher quality stock (paper) you use for brochures is better for printing photos on and everything looks, well, shinier.

By talking to your printer, you can create something genuinely lovely to touch. The sense of touch is probably the least well understood in terms of marketing communications effectiveness. Maybe because most agencies and clients only truly get excited by TV advertising, or press at a pinch. If you're selling high-end goods then something smooth, silky and stiff [*steady on – Ed.*] starts selling before your customer has read a word.

Brochures can be kept (or at least filed) when sales letters, ads and other ephemera have been consigned to the recycling box, to emerge again when your customer is in the mood to make that buying decision.

Because of their neutral tone of voice and production values, brochures can do duty in a variety of contexts. You can mail them, sure. But you can also give them out to people at exhibitions, sit them in a literature dispenser in your reception area or include them in a press kit, all uses that would sit a little oddly with a sales letter, for example.

Weaknesses

Because of the way many brochures are written and designed, they look pretty but are far less engaging than letters or good direct response advertising. So although you can use them in the contexts I listed above, it's not clear how much good they do. You're unlikely to get orders flooding in just because you scatter brochures around an exhibition hall like confetti. You really need that extra impetus that comes from a well-trained and enthusiastic sales person.

They are also expensive. If you're selling yachts then yes, I think you need a brochure. If you're selling magazine subscriptions, you may want a brochure to show off those double- or triple-page spreads of Hollywood's finest but I'm not sure you need one. A publishing client of mine has tested omitting brochures from her mailpacks and found no difference in response. Given the additional cost of including one, she now doesn't bother, and has improved her return on investment (ROI) in the process.

The fact that you can go on adding content to brochures means that many organisations end up saying everything, rather than the right thing. It's the printed equivalent of the sales person who never notices those buying signals because they're too busy talking, and keeps selling when they should be closing. The reader is overwhelmed with information, when what they're really looking for is reasons to buy.

What can you use it for?

Contextually speaking, you can use brochures to:

- Add information to a mailshot without padding the letter.
- Give sales people something to hand out to prospects (they often feel more motivated to get out there when you provide this sort of collateral).

- Warm up exhibition visitors.
- Inform journalists about your organisation and its products or services.
- Provide visitors to your premises with something to read while they're waiting.
- Lend weight to tenders you're submitting.

And, in their lighter, more toned guise of leaflets, you can use them as loose inserts in magazines or newspapers as part of a direct marketing campaign.

In terms of marketing applications, you can use them for:

- Generating sales leads.
- Winning orders.
- Driving free trials of your product.
- Improving people's perceptions of your organisation.
- Gaining new members or supporters.

What goes wrong

Over-written

Freed from the apparent need to connect with the reader, many copy-writers, when writing brochures, tend to kick back a bit. 'Ah!' they moan softly. 'At last … I can write. Really write!' The knuckles crack, the framed portrait of Raymond Chandler or Jane Austen seems to smile encouragingly down on them, and they're off. Into a field of prose so purple it's positively imperial. No sector is immune, but, once again, the car industry leads the field, particular for performance or luxury cars. (Though eco-cars are fast (slow?) becoming the third member of this over-written group.) You know the sort of thing…

Combining grace, a refined design aesthetic and a hunkered-down stance that bespeaks hidden depths of power, the Lexfinides Arcturion X920 boasts breathtaking performance and the largest cup-holders in its class.

61

Does anyone buy this? (The copy I mean, not the cars.) It looks increasingly out of touch in the age of the chat room and user forum, where manufacturers can, if they choose, discover what their *customers* are writing about their products.

Over-designed

If writers get all hot and bothered when a brochure comes up for discussion, wait till you see what happens to designers. All that space. All that freedom. All that budget! I've only met a couple of designers who enjoy laying out sales letters. Not enough to do, you see (or is there? See Chapter 2). But I've never met a designer who didn't enjoy doing brochures. There's something about the format that brings out designers' 'creativity'. Unfortunately, this can result in a piece that, while aesthetically pleasing, reduces the copy to the status of one of the 'wooden lords' in a Shakespeare history play. You know, the ones loitering at the back of the stage saying, 'My liege, what news from the Low Countries?'

Perhaps because few designers are taught typography any more, they tend to regard copy as an intrusion or, worse, an irrelevance, like the guest at a party who nobody else knows. So your words, so carefully crafted, get shoved against a wall, or tucked into the space between the kitchen and the downstairs toilet. In a sense this is really under-design, not over-design. White type reversed out of a black or coloured ground is terrible for anything that has to be read in daylight, yet it's a favourite of brochure designers. Tiny type doesn't work anywhere, ditto.

Not enough detail

If you're selling something expensive, like a motorbike, your prospect needs to feel that the emotional decision they've already made is buttressed by unassailable logic. In reality, they want to hack off down the Pacific Highway (or at least the North Circular) with the soundtrack to *Easy Rider* throbbing insistently inside their helmet. But they can't. Not until the head has followed the heart. It's because we are – or, rather, want to be – rational creatures. Shoes, gadgets, luxury foods: for many people with the money to afford them, the desire isn't enough. The internal finance director needs to be convinced that it's a *wise purchase*. And it's the detail that does it.

If you focus only on the emotional benefits of buying, you leave this huge gap unplugged. But if you include tables of data about dimensions (yes, it will fit in the garage, which will lower insurance premiums); fuel efficiency (well I know it's bigger than my last bike but it actually costs less to run); and performance (it's not that I want to go 170 mph, it's the mid range acceleration that will help me get out of trouble in a hurry that's important), your prospect can satisfy themselves that they have performed all the due diligence they need to go ahead and buy it.

Impenetrable copy

Because the brochure is often the place where you describe your product rather than sell it, there's a temptation to go into exhaustive technical detail on how it was designed and built and the technologies that allow it to do its work. The question is, do your readers care? Yes they want enough detail to allow them to rationalise their decision, but the key word in that condition is 'enough'. It doesn't happen all the time, but when a product's designers, developers or engineers have a hand in writing the copy for the brochure, you can almost guarantee that it will be over-written. Too technical, too wordy, too much information. Unless you're selling to engineers, in which case it's probably impossible to give them too much information.

Too much narrative copy

It's fine to open a brochure with a couple of narrative paragraphs (ie paragraphs like this one, in 'normal' sentences), but people are more likely to skim these and any others written in a similar style. You can help them by breaking paragraphs into shorter-than-normal blocks. Remember that although four or five-line paragraphs look OK on screen, they become daunting grey blocks when set in the narrow columns of a brochure.

What you must include

Given that brochures favour facts over feelings, you must include all the relevant facts about your product (or service). Remember that facts aren't necessarily the same as features. It might be a fact that an A-list movie star drives one of your cars. But they won't be sitting in it when Joe Average buys one at his local dealership. In essence, you need to give your reader all the relevant information they need to be confident in buying from you. That could include any or all of the following:

Product
- Physical dimensions
- Weight
- Materials
- Colour
- Performance data
- Benefits
- Options
- Cost
- Packaging
- Delivery method
- Environmental impact
- How it's made
- How it's tested
- Who else uses it
- What they say about it
- What happens if it goes wrong (not that it's going to but it's good to know)
- Photographs, illustrations, diagrams

Service
- Who provides the service
- Their qualifications
- What the service consists of
- Who it's aimed at

> Given that brochures favour facts over feelings, you must include all the relevant facts about your product (or service).

- Benefits
- The process for tailoring or specifying it
- What makes your service special
- Photographs, illustrations, diagrams

I mentioned digital print earlier. Now you can create personalised brochures that are specific to individual customers. An example: I wrote some copy for an American company's website a while ago. One of their services was managing the production of tailored brochures for car manufacturers. The manufacturer's sales staff would meet punters at a car show, collect their details including things like their ideal colour for a car, their hobbies, whether they had a family and so on. Let's say the customer prefers red, plays golf, has two children and is planning to buy them a dog. The sales representative then uploads this personal data to their print facility via the web. Two days later, the customer would receive a full colour brochure in the post featuring a red estate car on a golf course, with kids in the back seats and a Labrador sitting dutifully at its master's feet. Cool.

Copy gets personalised too, from a bank of paragraphs relevant to the distinct customer segments defined by the client. Your job is easy. You just have to plan your copy according to a grid of possibilities, rather than writing a single narrative aimed at a single, typical punter.

What you can leave out

You can leave out stuff that pleases you but won't make the punter more ready to buy from you. I'd say that would include the following:

Background copy that 'sets the scene' by, for example, describing the history of the printing press before trying to sell a multi-function desktop printer/copier/scanner.

Copy you've always wanted to write but never quite found the right vehicle for. Such as 'nature' copy, where you research some animal (it's always an animal, never a plant), force a connection with your product, then give it the full beans on a couple of hundred words of colourful creative writing that wouldn't be out of place in a wildlife magazine.

Your aspirations. Nobody cares whether you hope this will prove to be the most reliable widget since Fred T Barker first carved a crude widget from polymerised chicken dung in his shed. It either is, or it isn't.

Your emotions. Nor does anybody care what you feel about your product. Yes, I'm sure that after remortgaging your house, getting all your relations to buy £500 of shares each in your new company and working 70 hours a week for three years, you are delighted (not to say mightily relieved) that your product has finally come to market. But why should your prospects care? The big question is, will it solve their problems?

How to structure it

You may feel that long letters aren't right for your product, market or customers, and stick to one page, so the brochure is where you should tell the whole story, including all the features. So how do you persuade your potential customer to take their time and read it all? Here are a few practical ideas.

Use bullet points and lists

People love reading lists. They look less daunting and come with built-in white space, which gives your copy room to breathe. Use bullet points when the order of your list items isn't important, a numbered list when it is (perhaps a set of operating instructions, or 'how to order').

If you're using bullets, stick to one type – all circles or all dashes, squares, whatever. And *please* don't punctuate them as if they were a long narrative sentence, ie with semi-colons and a final full stop. The bullet points themselves do the job of splitting the items and the semi-colons just add clutter.

Have a Q&A section

I love these. They look so impartial, as if you're merely providing an information service. But, of course, *you* wrote the questions, so they lead into further selling copy in the guise of simple answers. You need to adopt a different tone of voice for these: wide-eyed but not overtly stupid for the Qs, authoritative and friendly for the As.

Use testimonials

I've written about these before, but they are *so* useful they deserve another airing. Whether you draft them or you let your customers do the hard work, make sure that the testimonials make a series of relevant points about your product. Try to be specific, rather than the '...I find Sunfish very useful in my work...' style. If your product saves people time, or makes them feel special, explain how.

Selling to a decision-making group

It often happens, perhaps it always happens, that you are never really selling to just one person. In business-to-consumer (b2c) copywriting, your punter is almost certain to discuss their purchase with a spouse, a friend or a relation. Or with other members of their favoured user group or chatroom. In business-to-business (b2b) copywriting, there may be formal arrangements for purchasing: you will often be faced with persuading the user (the ultimate consumer of your product), the specifier (who lays down the rules for purchasing it) and the authoriser (who holds the purse-strings and has final approval over the buying decision – which is really only a recommendation).

The question I'm often asked in training courses is, how do you speak to each person in the group in language that's relevant to them? And it's a good one. Unless you're going to mail them all separately with tailored versions of the brochure (not impossible, but not cheap either), you have to find a way to talk to each of them separately. Here's how I do it:

The bulk of the copy talks about the product rather than to the reader (I know, I know, it's not what I said before, but go with me).

The tone is still conversational, so it feels personal, but the benefits are generic. Then you have a section that looks like this:

Who should buy iWidget?

Accountants – who want greater control over widget costs
Engineers – who need to design custom widgets to tighter tolerances
Marketeers – who want to add value to clients' businesses
Investors – who need to track widget makers' shares in real time
Designers – who want to test new colours with web-based focus groups

This simple device (the list, not the iWidget) allows you to do two things: hook people in by saying, 'look this is for you' and show each group WHY they should be interested.

In terms of the broad structure of the brochure, it's pretty much the same as a press ad:

Headline
Introductory paragraph that introduces the product and delivers the knockout sales point (also known as the main benefit).

Second paragraph that expands on the benefit and maybe introduces proof. Or that raises and knocks flat the main objection (if it's serious enough).

Then one or more of the items from the 'What you must include' section above, laid out according to a coherent visual hierarchy and typographic scheme that draws your reader through the brochure to the order form/call to action.

The order form/call to action. If it's a form, have somebody who wasn't involved in writing or designing the brochure fill it in. Was it easy? Did they understand what they were ordering and how to go about it? Did anything confuse or irritate them? It's all valuable feedback and best done at the proof stage, not when you have 10,000 sitting in a mailing house somewhere. And please, don't put the words 'Order form' at the top. This is a little bugbear of mine. It's obviously an order form. Why waste space stating the obvious? Instead I recommend 'Order now'. Or 'Order within 14 days and get a FREE book'.

Notes on style and tone of voice

Although I always try to write copy in a personal, conversational style, when I'm writing brochures it does veer away from the ultra-personal style I'd use for an email or sales letter. You become a bit cooler, a bit more down to earth, a bit more neutral. The product is the hero. It can help to imagine you're a journalist writing a feature article about the product. How would *they* write the copy? They wouldn't gush, they wouldn't get frenziedly excited about its revolutionary new water filtration technology. They'd be dispassionate, analytical, calm.

> **Nobody buys this over-hyped style of copywriting any more.**

This style will work. I go back to the 'over-written' section above in 'What goes wrong'. Nobody buys this over-hyped style of copywriting any more. They're all too cynical, too heard-it-all-before, too web-savvy. So take the time and trouble to do your research and you'll find the hook, the angle you need to genuinely excite your reader.

When you're thinking about tone of voice, think first about who you're talking to. Engineers will not be impressed or engaged by a wildly enthusiastic tone – they tend to be cautious people, wary of unsubstantiated claims, keen to verify what they're told through controlled, repeatable experiment. So you need to be controlled, measured and relatively formal in tone. Surfers, on the other hand, may respond to a freer, more informal tone, but really, really watch your language. Any private argot, like surf slang, can mutate almost overnight: those trying to ingratiate themselves into the group by using the latest buzzwords can end up looking merely desperate. Gnarly, dude!

Using images

Your brochure is where you show the punter what you expect them to buy. This is no place for abstract arty images or the usual sad roster of good-looking executives and drops of water crowning upward from a mirror-like surface. Use sample pages/packshots/product shots with call-outs (you know, those little bits of text with arrows pointing to the relevant page) instead. Or use images that dramatise the benefits of the product. If you're flogging high-powered motorbikes to middle-aged men, they're *buying* a bike, but they're *paying* to be transported to a world where they are free (of mortgage worries, career worries, family worries, ageing worries). So show the bike by all means, but show it being leaned into a bend on a sweeping road without any other traffic, preferably somewhere dramatic like the Nevada desert.

If you're promoting a publication of any kind, use sample pages. Add a drop-shadow if you want to create a more three-dimensional feel and always use call-outs. People tend to look at picture captions (of which these are a special type) so they're an ideal place to put some stealth sales copy.

You should also use call-outs or captions with any kind of product shot or illustration. They needn't be merely descriptive either. You can reinforce your benefits copy in a call-out by not just labelling the image but explaining why that particular feature is good for the purchaser. You could say something like this:

> Titanium sprockets. Up to 55% lighter than conventional steel, these patented sprockets transform more of your muscle power into forward motion.

As with all the other chapters in this book, I recommend you commission or use original photography. Photographers aren't wildly expensive and good ones will be able to take a subject you find samey through overexposure and find a new angle (literally) that makes it look fresh and exciting.

As with all the other chapters in this book, I recommend you commission or use original photography.

**Figure 4 Brochure promoting
Sodexo's SayShopping Pass as a
Christmas staff incentive**

Light up their Christmas with
SayShopping Pass

SO YOU'RE CHOOSING that all-important Christmas
staff gift...

How can you make it personal, yet suitable for all your
employees? And, most importantly, something that will
boost their loyalty and motivation?

Staff Motivation
isn't just for Christmas...

SayShopping Pass is so much more than
another spend-it-and-forget-it voucher or
cash gift. It's a passport to over 60 specially
-selected "brand champions" with 12,000
outlets between them nationwide.

What's more, with no ties to a single retailer,
SayShopping Pass can be enjoyed by everyone – whatever they like, however they want
to treat themselves.

...here's a rewarding way to
make it last all year

Your staff will value the effort you've put into
selecting their Christmas gift. And the treat
they give themselves will always be linked to
you and your business. So they feel rewarded
AND motivated.

Copy broken up into manageable
chunks, integrated with the design
concept, and, because it was a
Christmas promotion, a few slightly
corny lines.

(See over for the call to action.)

Underneath all the colour was
a strong sales message that led
the reader through to the call
to action.

CHAPTER 6
PRESS AD

NOW, THE SIMPLE COPYWRITING TECHNIQUE THAT STOPS PEOPLE TURNING THE PAGE

Introduction

This chapter is about press advertising, which doesn't on the face of it seem to need a definition as such. I should make clear that my experience is principally in direct response advertising – that is, advertising designed expressly to make a sale. So-called brand advertising has a vaguer goal, but there's no reason why it shouldn't have to perform to the same stringent criteria as its less glamorous cousin.

If you're going to write a press ad, you have one very important decision to make before you do anything else. Answer this question.

What is the ad for?

And *please*, if your answer is 'to raise awareness,' put your pen down and cancel that space order. Why? Simply this. Where do you intend to raise awareness from? And where to? Because if you don't know, how on earth are you going to measure the impact of your ad? And if you can't measure it, how will you know whether your money was well spent?

Now, of course, I know that the theory is you just advertise like hell and rely on the cumulative effect of all those repetitions to bring in sales at some point. (Because let's remember, that is the ultimate point of advertising.) But the people you'll most often find peddling that line come from two groups you could hardly call disinterested. One, advertising agencies, who make fat commissions (still) on media spend and handsome creative fees on bombastic campaigns that just have to have double pages in the Financial Times. Two, ad sales executives. See above re. commission.

Strengths

The main strength or advantage of a press ad is that it's carried right into your prospect's home – or office – within something they care about: their daily newspaper or a magazine. This Trojan Horse effect overcomes one of the big hurdles facing every type of

> What is the ad for? And please, if your answer is 'to raise awareness,' put your pen down and cancel that space order.

copywriting – getting past your prospect's inertia/spam filter/ hostility. So, you get a free ride into the citadel. There are pitfalls, of course, and we'll come onto those shortly, but you can be reasonably certain that your prospect will at the very least *see* your ad.

Depending on your budget, you also have a great deal of space to play with. A full-page in a broadsheet newspaper let alone a double-page spread (DPS) is an almost unimaginably large piece of real estate for a copywriter. Perhaps that's why so many seem to crack up under the strain and write 20 words of copy and leave the rest to the art director to fill in with a photo of a banana and then leave the rest blank.

You also have the option of full colour, and in glossy magazines really high quality reproduction for photos and the possibility of linking your ad to loose or bound-in inserts, tip-ons and various other creative solutions dreamt up by the magazine's advertising department.

Weaknesses

The main weakness of press advertising is the flipside of its strength. Yes, it gets carried into your prospect's home or workplace, but most people don't buy newspapers and magazines in order to read ads. So the Trojan Horse rolls to a stop inside the city walls, the hatch opens and out pour the Greeks. Only to find there's nobody there.

Most ads signal their irrelevance to the reader by using a set of advertising conventions that almost scream, 'you didn't pay for this and it's nothing to do with the editorial'. Think about your own reading behaviour when you're settling down with your favourite magazine. You probably flip through once, scanning for interesting articles or pictures. Each time you come to a page of advertising you turn the page, probably without even reading the headline. Because you *know* it's an ad.

The other weakness of press advertising is its crippling expense. Or to be more precise, the cripplingly precarious relationship between what you spend on it and what you can measurably conclude you made from it. A phrase attributed to Lord Leverhulme, the founder of Lever Brothers, ultimately to become Unilever, went, 'Half the money I spend on advertising is wasted, and the problem is I do not know which half'. The problem for today's advertisers is more serious even than that, I think. They may well be wasting *all* of their advertising budget, since they never track, record or measure the response they get.

A final weakness of press advertising, and this is not a piece of special pleading, is that much if not most of it is produced by advertising agencies. Many of them tend to think in terms of brand awareness or 'impact', rather than cold, hard cash, and that leads them to produce advertising that pleases the client on aesthetic grounds, yet leaves the reader unmoved. Perhaps because there is very rarely much meat to get your teeth into to help you decide whether to buy the product being advertised. I have been told on several occasions by marketeers on my training courses that as the exercise involves writing copy for a press ad, 'It's got to be really short'. Hmmm.

What can you use it for

OK. Let's start again. You're running an ad because you want to achieve measurable business results. Here are 21 objectives you might have for your ad. You want people to...

1. Join your professional association
2. Subscribe to your newsletter or e-zine
3. Stay at your hotel
4. Request a free trial of your product
5. Register for your website
6. Order your market intelligence service
7. Try your new magazine
8. Sign up to your satellite TV channel
9. Give you their wine collection to look after

10. Come along to an event
11. Visit your health club
12. Get their car serviced at your garage
13. Insure their art collection with you
14. Become a member of your social networking site
15. Buy your book
16. Hire you as their consultant
17. Call you to book a coaching session
18. Reserve a place at your conference
19. Advertise in your newspaper
20. Invest in your business
21. Send their children to your nursery

Fantastic. All measurable. And all totally suitable for press advertising.

What goes wrong

Too 'ad-y'

Most press ads fall down because they look – and sound – 'ad-y'. They look like other ads, which is bad because it lets the reader see at a glance that they're not part of the magazine they paid for. Worse still, they fail to devote enough space to the selling message, relying instead on overly arty layouts where abstract or non-related pictures dominate the layout, with the copy reduced to a bit-part.

Not enough copy

If all you want to do is raise awareness of your product, service or company, then a few words will surely do it. Writing 'XYZ Company and its products are crap' will certainly achieve your objectives, and in just seven words. But if you want to part someone from their money then you'll generally find it pays to write a little more. Enough, in fact, to answer all their questions, both positive, 'What's in it for me?' and negative, 'What if it all goes wrong?'

Too much white space

White space plays a vital role in advertising. It can, if used correctly, draw the eye to key parts of the copy or graphics, or provide breathing space for the copy. But this is a far cry from the acres of expensive media space left blank merely to satisfy the art director's artistic pretensions. A simple test: if the copy is so small you can't read it easily, there's too much white space. (Assuming you haven't filled every square centimetre already.)

Pictures leading the copy

I once ran a copywriting seminar for some companies in the construction industry. To make it relevant to their business I pulled a few ads from the main trade journal. The one I remember most clearly had, for its illustration, a teacup, above which loomed a menacing black cloud, with rain lashing down and a bolt of lightning zig-zagging into the tea. The headline? Ready? All together now…

A Storm in a Teacup

Give the reader a
reason to buy from you.

Regretfully, but not altogether surprisingly, I can't remember what the ad was promoting. This sort of lame-brained advertising breaks the cardinal rule: that the image should agree with the proposition, not the headline. In fact it's worse, because you can't help feeling that the headline – a honker of a cliché to begin with – was only chosen because the hapless copywriter was already envisioning the accompanying photo.

No obvious reason to take the desired action

A lot of press ads forget one of the most basic copywriting rules: give the reader a reason to buy from you. In simple terms that means talking about benefits. Or you can think of it as making an appeal to the reader's self-interest. That might mean guilt, or greed, or fear, or lust, or laziness or the desire to save money, provide for your family or get a better job.

No call to action

When you're in sales, it pays – literally – to ask for the order. So why do so many press ads slip up on this fundamental point? I suspect there's a certain breed of advertising copywriter who finds the whole idea of selling – in fact commerce in general – a little distasteful. They can knock out their brand-building ads while working on that screenplay or novel, where their heart really lies, and for which their degree in English literature or film studies prepared them. At any rate, short of the ads for baked beans or loo paper, where even the doziest consumer can work out they're supposed to go to their local supermarket or convenience store to pick up a pack, you should include an explicit call to action, with phone number, website, email address and number to text.

Me-too ideas

There's a raft of ideas you will see over and over in press ads. A short, non-exclusive collection would include bemused or puzzled-looking businessman; Dalmatian dog but with unusually shaped or coloured spots; all the copy reversed out of black, or worse, a photograph: girls in their underwear; Formula 1 racing cars... and so on.

Maybe sitting down and thinking hard about how their product would benefit the prospect is too much for these writers. So they fall back on the vast ragbag of easily visible ideas (lame or otherwise) and choose one of those to copy. Trouble is, they didn't work for the first people to try them, so what's the point?

What you must include

When you write a press ad, try to include all the things you'd include in a sales letter or an HTML email (assuming that these aren't brief spurts of hype). A checklist might look like this:

• How what you're selling makes your prospect's life easier. In detail.

- Answers to any objections the typical prospect might have. Is it more expensive than other, similar products? Explain why.
- Evidence that what you're saying is true. Statistics, endorsement or case studies work here.
- Reassurance – customer testimonials or third-party endorsements work well.
- A picture. Either the thing you're selling, or something that dramatises its main benefit.
- A call to action, as discussed above, with full details of how to order or take the desired action.

The point about press ads is that, apart from the fact of the medium itself and any production constraints, it's not much different, as copy, from any other sort of sales piece. The same people are reading it – those interested in what you're selling; and they're reading it for the same reasons – because you appear to have something that meets a need they have. So writing in a different style to a sales letter or web page, or including completely different content, is a curious decision.

What you can leave out

Cut anything that leaves your reader unmoved. So, long-winded descriptions of your company and its mission or values... detailed descriptions of what your product is, rather than what it does... beautiful but irrelevant passages describing, for example, the way the eye works, how an octopus swims or the history of evolution ... superlatives and hype-words including but not limited to exciting, fantastic, unique, revolutionary, amazing, groundbreaking, incredible.

How to structure it

A line at the very top that calls to your target reader.
If are writing an ad aimed at homemakers, for a new type of flour perhaps, you could simply say:

Attention busy home cooks…

That will ensure all busy home cooks pause long enough to read the next line, which is…

The headline
I've covered headlines in greater detail in Chapter 1, but to recap a few basic points…

- 'Teaser' headlines only work if they also promise a benefit. People are too busy for puzzles. If they want to solve puzzles, they buy puzzle magazines or do Sudoku.
- In general, headlines need to be brief. Let's stick to 10-16 words. Use a subhead if you really must say more up top.
- Remember, headlines are there to stop your reader from turning the page, outline your promise in short, and encourage them to read on.

For our flour, the headline could say:
How to make light-as-air sponge cakes… every time

A sub-head
You can use a sub-head to draw the reader in still further or introduce a new element such as a special offer or premium:
Professional bakers swear by Wonderlight flour. Try it for yourself with this free 100g trial pack

Body copy
The body copy is where you make your case. And your sale. The structure of the copy in a press ad mirrors that for a sales letter. You

start with the main appeal, expand on it, prove it, introduce reassurance, make them want it and finally ask for the order.

The opening

Joseph Sugarman, the US mail order copywriter, contends that your first sentence is there *only* to make the reader read the second sentence. And that the second sentence must make the reader read the third. The third, the fourth, and so on. His rule is that your first sentence must be short and simple. There's no challenge to the reader's intellect or powers of concentration. The message of the first sentence isn't, 'buy this product' – it's 'read this ad'. And because Joe makes his opening sentences so easy to read, the reader does just that. By the end of the ad, they do buy the product, which is the message of the *whole* ad.

So, for our Wonderlight ad, the first sentence could read, 'It's heavy.' Home cooks know that feeling as they pull a cake from the oven, or cut into it. It begins to make the case for both reading on *and* the Wonderlight flour. The second and third sentences might expand on the first like this: 'We've all had that sinking feeling. Why didn't it rise like it did last time?' Then we could lead the reader gently, towards the pitch. 'Was it the creaming? The temperature? The flour?' If they are still with you at this point, they have read past six sentence-ends: two full stops and four question marks. That means you have trained them remarkably quickly to read your copy.

Objection handling

In the body of your ad copy you must cover all the reasons why they should buy from you: the benefits of your product. And all the reasons why they might not buy from you: their objections. If an objection is so important that it stands between you and a sale, you need to raise it straight away, and then resolve it. You know what to say because when you planned your copy, you would have made a list of all the objections and how you were going to counter them.

Now, shall we talk about copy length for a moment?

> Your first sentence is there only to make the reader read the second sentence.

Long copy

Surprisingly, to lay people at least, ten-word ads rarely out-pull 100-word ads on the same brief. And 100-word ads rarely out-pull 1,000-word ads. 'I can't believe people would read that much copy,' they say. But they do. Testing reveals the truth. You can bury an offer for a premium of some kind deep in the body copy and you *will* get redemptions. Here's why it works.

The *only* people who are going to buy from you are the people who are *already* interested in what you have to sell. Keen gardeners are interested in defeating slugs. Petrolheads are interested in fast cars. Quality control managers are interested in methods of minimising defects. CEOs are interested in maximising shareholder value (let's not forget why – they have huge stock options). So if you offer them an ad headed:

The new scientifically proven method of keeping your flowerbeds slug free
Your chance to sit behind the wheel of an Aston Martin
Take production line defects below 0.01%
Put a smile on the face of your shareholders

… they will want to know more. Much more. As much as you can tell them. Why only give them half or a quarter of the story? You wouldn't in a sales letter so why do it in an ad? 'Because ads have to be short,' is the deafening response. 'Ads aren't supposed to sell, they're just there to raise awareness.' And, finally, 'Ads have to be ads.' There is a way out of this circle of shameful reasoning and that's simply to start a rigorous programme of testing. Write two ads, one short and one long, run them as an A/B test and just count the orders. You might, just, find that short outperforms long, in which case you can stop wasting time bashing out 2,000-word ads and go for lunch. But it's far *more* likely that you'll discover something all the great mail order companies, fundraisers and magazine publishers have known for years (and, to be fair, *not* kept to themselves), which is that long copy works better.

So, write *everything* you can think of that will make your sale.

Benefits will always catch your reader's interest. And stop your ears against the honeyed words of those who whisper of 'more impact with a bigger image', or the 'dramatic use of white space'. I pulled out two ads from my Museum of Pride (it's a small museum, housed on the head of a pin; unlike my Museum of Shame, which occupies a large barn on the outskirts of Salisbury) and counted the words (easier than counting the neighbouring angels).

The first, for Bill Fryer Direct – a direct marketing agency – had 330 words of body copy. The second, for Google, had 357. Go figure. Incidentally, both had headlines beginning, 'How…'.

Reassurance

As you work through your body copy, you should include a testimonial or two, or three. They break up the text and allow you to introduce some independent witnesses who'll vouch for the effectiveness of your product. Perhaps you or your company or your product has won an award for customer service or innovation or product excellence. If you have, mention it and reproduce the award logo. Or favourable press coverage. Anything, really, that sends a message to your prospect that you are a reputable company with a product to match. If you offer a money-back guarantee, you should definitely mention this. Mark it off under a separate heading, or put it in a panel. Get your designer to create a certificate border or seal to add credibility. Ultimately, the credibility comes from your copy, though. Something like this:

> I am so sure that Wonderlight will give you perfect sponge cakes every time, I want to give you this PERSONAL guarantee. If you decide, after baking with Wonderlight, that it doesn't live up to my promise, simply return the packet top (you can keep the flour) and I will refund the entire purchase price. No questions asked.

Call to action

Some people like to start writing ads by writing the call to action. It's straightforward and gets your wheels turning. Tell them what you want them to do. It will get you into the right frame of mind for the rest of the ad. And this is no time for pussyfooting around. Use the imperative mood. Instruct your reader to do the thing you want them to.

Give them a deadline. Give them an incentive. Give them a simple way to respond. And if you're using a coupon, aim for as few cuts as possible to get it out of the publication it appears in. Nobody has time for paper sculpture these days so centred octagonal order forms are out.

Provide phone, email, web and postal response channels. Let people choose. But be aware that when it comes to the order itself, simplicity is best. The more choices they have to make, the lower the response. That goes for product choice and payment methods. Though it is orthodoxy in some quarters to offer cheque, credit card, Direct Debit or invoice methods, research has shown that this depresses response. A straight 'bill me' option for payment will maximise response, though you will then have to write a billing series (multiple letters chasing payment) to get the money in. You will also have to write off a certain proportion of your orders as bad debts.

Notes on style and tone of voice

I have identified three broad styles of advertising copywriting style.

Style 1 – ads trying to sell stuff to consumers. These vary in the specifics of their style – a luxury watch is a consumer product as much as a tin of beans is, but they use different tones of voice. But they are all understandable and attempt to engage the reader on their own level.

Style 2 – ads trying to sell stuff to business people. The so-called business-to-business (b2b) school of copywriting tends to be dull, worthy, inflated with woolly jargon and 'strategic' phrase-making that can only leave the reader cold. Luckily these firms also have salespeople and account managers who can actually shift inventory.

Style 3 – corporate advertising. God help us, but this is the most impenetrable, self-aggrandising, *painful* school of copywriting ever devised. The best place to find great examples of the style is within the pages of the *Financial Times*, *The Economist* or any of the other high-end business publications.

If you are paying – handsomely – for advertising space, wouldn't it make sense to try to connect with the people likely to be reading the publication where your ad will appear? That means using down to earth language that doesn't require a dual-core processor to understand. I imagine many writers of styles 2 and 3 above don't, won't or can't master this simple approach because they have never paused in their labours long enough to imagine what it might be like to be on the receiving end of their own copy. Having hung around with all sorts of people over the years, from crane drivers to chief executives, I can confidently assert that *nobody talks like that!*

On the assumption that your sales letters are written in a plain English, engaging style where you try to establish rapport with your reader and offer simple solutions to their problems, use that approach for your ads too. And forget about how many readers the publication has. When your reader reads your copy, they are not part of a crowd, hanging adoringly on your words like cult members: they are alone.

Using images

I have some pretty fixed views – prejudices, really – about fatuous advertising imagery. (You may not agree with me, of course.) Here's what I think *works*.

• Pictures of your product.
• Pictures of your customers using your product.
• Pictures of people who are like your reader. (So that's no more bikini-girls for the building trade, then.)

• Pictures that show how the reader's fortunes will improve if they buy from you.
• Pictures that dramatise the benefits of your product.

And here's what I think *doesn't* work.

Cheetahs, dolphins, sharks, chessmen, handshakes, clocks, businessmen, groups of models balanced for age, gender, ethnicity and so forth, punks, storms in teacups, cute animals, smiling telephone operators... well, you get the picture.

If you do decide to include an image, make sure it agrees with the proposition. In other words, if you promise people they will save money fast, show them an image that means saving money. Not, because you like the idea of a headline reading, 'Faster than a speeding bullet' a picture of a man in a Superman outfit.

I have lost count of the number of ads for solicitors, accountants and other professional firms based on the idea of service, where the headline reads, variously:

We bend over backwards to help you
We go the extra mile
We're your number one fan

illustrated by, in turn:

Man bending over backwards
Man running past milepost
Man holding cheerleader pom-poms

Come on guys! We can do better than this.

Figure 5 Press ad for Cert Octavian's wine storage business, Octavian Cellars.

'The idea of the advert was to get prospects to think 'where is my wine?' as storage is mostly arranged by their merchant, who does not necessarily store in the best place. As far as the advert itself, the photograph was the starting point and in my view it does double duty – keeps attention and reinforces confidence due to the quality of the image.

The headline was designed to generate curiosity, and questions make people think about the subject.'

Nigel Jagger, Chairman, Cert Octavian plc

"Why wouldn't you want to store your wine perfectly in the safest place on Earth?"

LAURIE GREER, CELLAR MASTER AT CORSHAM CELLARS

Provenance pays

It is a fact that perfectly stored wine demands a higher price. Which could be why 10,000 wine collectors from 39 countries choose to store their collections at the world's leading storage facility.

Unsurpassed environment

Corsham Cellars lie 100 feet below the Bath stone hills of Wiltshire. Crucially, this depth not only eliminates natural light and vibration, it provides optimum temperatures and constant humidity. Or, more simply, perfect cellarage. And it's the only commercially accessible facility on earth where you'll find it.

Security and integrity

So, perfect conditions are paramount. But it's also vital that a storage facility is financially secure and has unquestioned integrity. Fortunately for the collections within Corsham Cellars, they are protected by the financial strength of Cert Octavian – a distinction that matters when laying down wine for a number of years.

Invaluable service

You may decide you do not require such levels of care. In which case, perhaps the last words on the subject should be left to Laurie himself: "There is nothing quite so soul-destroying as opening

a priceless bottle of wine only to discover it has been ruined by poor storage. It is a travesty." We couldn't agree more.

For more information on Octavian Vaults, our premium wine storage service at Corsham Cellars, call Laurie Greer on 01225 818714 or email him on cellar.master@certoctavian.co.uk

OCTAVIAN VAULTS
THE FINEST WINE CELLARAGE

www.octavianvaults.co.uk

Figure 6 Press ad for Streetwise Publications' 'The Driver's Survival Handbook'.

'Marketeers tend to get bored with their ads quicker than their customers. I'm more than happy to leave an ad to run while it's still making money. This is partly laziness (writing copy is always painful) but mainly the realisation that there's no point in fixing what isn't broken.

Having said that, we've tested a number of alternatives over the years (there may be something better) but they've never beaten the control. The only things we've changed are the testimonials and the picture.'

John Harrison, Streetwise Publications

CHAPTER 7
PRESENTATION

AS YOU CAN SEE ON THIS SLIDE...

Introduction

I use it. You use it. I've been to a christening where the priest used it. (Truly, I have.) But do we really need it? And if we do, are we using it correctly? Here are some of the reasons why a lot of people use Microsoft® Office PowerPoint (and its competitors):

a) It's a substitute for original thought.
b) It's a crutch for the nervous.
c) It's a great way to pass an afternoon.
d) It's there.
e) It looks slick.
f) It appears to save time.

The best presentation I ever saw was devoid of P. (Let's just call it P from now on – it saves time.) The speaker – an entertaining and knowledgeable Irishman called Barry Mahon – simply stood in front of the audience and spoke, without notes. With nothing else to look at or be distracted by, every member of the audience focused on Barry – and on what he was saying. I suspect this was his intention.

If you are going to use P, here are a few thoughts on making it work for you (and, more importantly, your audience), rather than the other way around. First, take a clean piece of white paper and a pencil. Now…

1. State your business goal. In other words, what are you trying to achieve? Is it an order? Senior management buy-in? Behaviour change in employees?
2. Identify and research your audience. Who are they? What do you know about them? Most important of all, how much do they know about the thing you'll be talking about? This will help you pitch your presentation at the right level.
3. Specify your objectives. What do you want your audience to know, feel and commit at the end of your presentation? Make them SMART objectives: Specific, Measurable, Achievable, Relevant and Timed.

4. Interrogate your product, service or idea. Make sure you fully understand it – especially from your audience's perspective.

5. Brainstorm ideas. Go for quantity not quality at this stage. You can filter them later.

6. Structure your presentation.

Now, if you must, launch P.

P use is now so widespread that in certain management consultancies, everything is written using it, even proposals. People like its apparent flexibility and pre-built presentations. It *is* a useful communications tool – *if* it's used properly. It's just that so many people don't. You can tell I'm not a huge fan, but here goes...

Strengths

First, a confession: I have used presentation software for almost every single presentation I have ever given. Though I am trying to wean myself off it, using fewer and fewer slides with each go. There's something terrifying about the thought of every member of your audience looking at you the whole time. What if your nose itches (or worse)? What if you forget your next point? And so on.

P does help you speak without notes. Though from my experience on both ends of presentations, virtually all speakers have notes as *well*.

More to the point, it allows you to present multimedia content. Very occasionally you'll see a presentation where the presenter has used P to deliver moving pictures, audio, animation (and not just slide transitions) and photographs or illustrations. Another presentation I'm glad I saw was given by a guy called Max McKeown. Max used P creatively – he didn't have his speech on screen, but he did show us TV ads, graphs and all sorts of thought-provoking images.

P also provides the basis for leave-behinds such as workbooks and sales folders. You just press a button and it spits all the slides out into your word processor.

And it can be very helpful if you use it for training courses. You can ensure everyone is thinking about the same point as you talk around the subject.

Weaknesses

The main weakness of Powerpoint is that it has become, through its ubiquity, a cliché of business life.

I'll try to stay calm. The main weakness of P is that it has become, through its ubiquity, a cliché of business life (and many other lives besides). Your heart sinks as you enter a meeting room dominated by a drop-down screen: you can already feel your will to live slipping away as the presenter gets onto their hind legs and clicks for the first of what will undoubtedly be 250 slides of increasingly unreadable text and baffling flowcharts. Oops, I said I'd try to stay calm.

P becomes an aim in itself. For many presenters, the bulk of the work is done simply in writing the presentation. Little or no thought goes into the desired response from the audience; or, more to the point, how sitting through the presentation will affect the likelihood of their doing it at all.

And because you write a P presentation on a computer screen but then deliver it on a much larger one (usually), there's often a mismatch between the ease of reading for the writer and the audience. We've all sat through presentations where the presenter has essentially typed a speech into P and then proceeded to read it out from the screen.

This leads to a further weakness, in that the presenter, having committed themselves to so much verbiage on screen, feels unable to tear themselves away from it, and delivers most of the presentation facing backwards.

What can you use it for

In theory, you can use P to help present anything. A short and definitely non-exhaustive list would include the following:

- training courses
- sales proposals
- research findings
- lessons or lectures
- product demonstrations
- sales briefings
- design proposals
- religious services

What goes wrong

Too many words/points

Perhaps because they want to order their thoughts, or give themselves something to read from on-screen, many people cram everything they want to *say* onto the slide. The resulting splatter of bullet points is too much for anyone to take in quickly and your audience will spend the whole time reading off the screen instead of listening to you.

Too much animation

I'm talking about slide builds and transitions here, rather than you showing old cartoons. How much is too much? It's *all* too much! I once sat through a half-hour presentation where the presenter had clearly spent ten times that long inserting every single slide transition and text-build effect from the P tool box into his presentation. If you stopped concentrating and just watched, it was quite fun, hypnotic really, as each new bullet point and slide faded, slid, pixellated, spiralled, bounced and zoomed into view. I can't remember anything he said, mind you.

Just because it's there doesn't mean you have to use it. Children might find it all very jolly, but unless you're presenting to children, and jollity is your main aim, I'd avoid it all.

Unreadable text

This is a problem for many communications channels, not just presentations. Poorly thought-out colour combinations, e.g. yellow on white or red on green (I've seen both), tiny type (see point 1 above) and dense paragraphs of copy: all surface on P slides and all make your audience's job impossible. But give people text on screen and they *will* persist in trying to read it. The resulting drain on their core processors will leave them with little or no memory left for whatever you're saying.

Over-complex charts and graphics

Designing P slides at your PC or Mac means you're viewing it from about 30-50 cm away from the screen. That allows you to create quite detailed, fiddly charts and graphics. However, project them onto a screen 5-30 metres away and, again, you've just thrown your audience a curveball.

What you must include

Writing a presentation is no different from writing a sales letter, press ad or email. You have to have a plan and at the top of your plan you need to have a goal. What are you trying to communicate? What response are you trying to get from your audience? That plan will drive your content. But do try to vary the way you communicate your ideas and messages. Use pictures as well as words. Use music, or video files.

In conceptual terms, you must include, or make, all the points that you need to for your audience to accept your proposal. If you're selling, that will include the features of the product or service, but much more importantly, the benefits these confer on the reader. You'll also want to include some sort of proof that your product does what you say it does, That could be statistics from your user base or customers. It could be case studies or testimonials. But remember at all times, that you are writing for the screen, so keep it brief. Ultra-brief. If you have some great testimonials, rather than type them all up and project them on screen, you could have a slide with a smiling face and a single line reading: 'Happy customers' then tell your audience you are going to read out a couple of testimonials.

If you are presenting research findings, of course you will want to show the headline figures or concepts you tested. But avoid the temptation to put every last multivariate analysis table up there. Instead, use the slides to cue in your next point and then tell your audience about the detailed findings.

Most people screw up presentations not because they are poor writers but because they are poor presenters. The paralysing anxiety many people experience when told they have to give a presentation is what drives them to overpopulate the slides. But there is an alternative (and as this isn't a book about presentation skills I'll leave off a general discussion about what you need to do to be a more confident presenter). You use the notes field below the slide. This is where you type up your speaker's notes, *not* on the slide itself. Then when you print your slides out for yourself, you get a neat set of bullet points *nobody can see except you.* Or use Presenter View. *These* are what you use to stay on track and confident you're not going to miss anything out.

And avoid the temptation to use your slides as handouts unless they *really* work as handouts. Instead, prepare handouts separately, maybe using a word processing program. You can include a copy of your slides for reference but there's no golden rule laid down anywhere that says you must. It all goes back to your plan. You should think of P as three discrete applications:

1 The on-screen presentation – designed to keep your audience focused and on track but essentially primed to *listen.*
2 The speaker notes – designed to keep *you* on track.
3 The leave behind – designed to remind your audience of your main points and encourage them to take the desired action.

> **Most people screw up presentations not because they are poor writers but because they are poor presenters.**

What you can leave out

I guess, by now, you know what I think you should leave out of a presentation. Like many of the other channels and formats discussed in this book, the high-concept answer is 'anything that doesn't move your audience closer to your objective'. The more practical answer is 'anything that distracts your audience from what you are saying and trying to get them to internalise, believe or remember'. That would include unnecessary animation, excessive text on-screen and tedious background descriptions of your company and its 'customer-facing solutions'.

How to structure it

To a large degree, the structure of your presentation depends on what you are trying to achieve and the style and purpose of your presentation. A sales presentation will have a different structure to an academic presentation. Or will it? Can we arrive at a generic structure that works in most cases? How about this.

You open with a brief statement of why you're there in front of your audience.

You move on to outline the problem or challenge or point of your presentation and, in outline, your answer. Do you have a better way of cleaning municipal drains? A new technology for creating presentations online? An answer to urban violence? A new proposal for teaching maths to 11-year-olds?

You go on to explain why your answer is better than any other. Why your hypothesis is more believable. Why your product is worth investing in. Why your research is worth taking further. That means detail.

You provide some objective proof or endorsement, in the form of statistics, testimonials, endorsements, citations, awards or press coverage.

You close with some kind of call to action. Don't just leave them dangling with a limp, 'well that's about it, really'. Ask for feedback, an order, the chance to provide a quotation or proposal.

However you structure your presentation in terms of slide order, here's the one *huge* point you must always remember...

Your audience isn't interested in you and they're certainly not interested in sitting through a boring presentation for an hour and a half.

No. They're interested in themselves. In how to solve the problem that's bugging them. A bit like with proposals and bid documents, they don't want to sit through a long screed about you, your company and your wonderful products. They want to hear how you are going to fix things for them. So when you're writing a presentation, bear this simple fact in mind. The best sales letters and emails always start by appealing to the reader's self-interest. In building rapport with the reader. In involving them in what you're saying. The same goes for presentations. The first thing I do when I am delivering a copywriting workshop is not to start flashing slides in front of people. I ask them to tell me about themselves and their burning issues about copywriting. Instant buy-in.

Notes on style and tone of voice

When using P itself, here are a few guidelines that I try to follow. You might find them helpful too.

- Follow the six-by-six rule for text slides. This means a maximum of six bullet points and six words per bullet.
- Try to emulate the style you find in newspaper headlines. Not grammatically complete sentences but packed with meaning.
- Avoid emotional language and anything that gives your text 'personality'. That's what *you're* there for.
- Ensure you use a point size that will be legible from the back

Used well, and creatively, Powerpoint can help you convince or inform people. But it should come last in the writing process, not first.

of the room in which you'll be presenting.

- Decide from the outset whether you are going to add full stops to your bullet points. If you do, use them consistently all the way through your presentation. If you don't, ditto.
- Avoid that ghastly and prissy use of semi-colons at the end of bullet points, except the penultimate one, where you often see a semi-colon followed by 'and', leading to the final bullet, which does end in a full stop.
- Avoid two-line slide titles or bullets: they are very demanding on your audience.
- Obvious this, but proofread your presentation, including running spell-check.

Used well, and creatively, P can help you convince or inform people. But it should come last in the writing process, not first. I suspect that 99% of all presentations delivered this year would be at least as effective without it, with the speaker instead using 5 x 7 index cards to speak to and engaging the audience with some emotion, eye contact and good old-fashioned salesmanship.

Using images

Great! Yes, use images. And make them moving images if you can. Be aware that the perfect little 72 dpi postage-stamp image you grabbed off the web may look awful once it's blown up to a metre across. On which subject, just because an image is on the web doesn't mean you have the right to use it. It may be subject to copyright. (You often find images have so-called watermarks across them if they are from commercial image libraries.) There are some very good and very cheap royalty-free image libraries on the web nowadays, where you can buy high-quality images for a few pounds. Three I have used are Shutterstock, iStockphoto and Fotolia.

If you do decide to use images, the same general rules apply to this format as to all the others. Make sure your image is there to communicate, not merely decorate. Make sure it isn't a cliché (no more businessmen shaking hands please). Make sure it is relevant and understandable to your audience.

Snap, crackle and pop

- Use power words for emotional kick.
- Use verbs not nouns.
- Use positive language.
- Use the active voice when you can.
- Use Anglo-Saxon, not Latin/Greek.

Write for results

Figure 7 Presentation slide from Write for Results, the business writing training company co-founded by the author

Try to follow the six by six rule for presentations – no more than six bullet points and six words per point. (This fails.)

Remember, the slides are there to help your audience, not you.

CHAPTER 8
E-ZINE

HI FRED, IT'S A BUSY MONTH HERE AT ACME CORPORATION

Introduction

Publishing an e-zine is a relatively cheap way of staying in touch with a big group of people who might either be customers or turn into them. It's an excellent way to enhance your reputation and keep your name in front of people. But there's a lot of 'em about. So yours needs to deliver standout content, and be easy, even entertaining, to read.

An e-zine exemplifies the 'give to get' marketing strategy so beloved of the current generation of marketing consultants. In the old days you paid for vast swathes of expensive media then filled it with self-aggrandising advertising messages (the argument goes). Customers were somehow tricked or bullied into buying from you under this relentless onslaught of hype. Now, in the internet age, there's a new 'paradigm' in town. Instead of promoting, we educate. Instead of pushing messages we pull customers to our sites. Instead of pitching we offer information.

It's hard to think of a business that doesn't want to build better relationships with its customers – whether in the business-to-consumer (b2c) or business-to-business (b2b) space – and from purely personal experience, I've not come across a more effective tool (barring lunch) for doing that than the e-zine. Let's venture on a definition of the term. An e-zine is a free, regular newsletter, delivered via email, to a group of people who have asked you to send it to them. Each of those six elements of the definition bears some analysis.

1. It's free: which, counter-intuitively, means it has to deliver more value than if it was paid for. Why? Well, because it was so easy to get it's just as easy to get rid of. Once people have paid for something, they'll spend a while convincing themselves that it's worth something. To do otherwise would be to admit they made a mistake with money, which people are loath to do.

2. It's regular: without a predictable pattern and reasonably frequent delivery (say no less often then monthly) the recipients fail to connect with it and fail to recognise it as part of their relationship with you and/or your organisation.

3. It's a newsletter: not a sales letter (though you will be doing some selling, both overt and covert). That means it should deliver news. Not necessarily topical, up-to-the-minute news – there's the web for that. Not even corporate news – much beloved of old-school corporate newsletter editors/writers, where every 'exciting' purchase of a Verbmeister 2750 lexical composition engine was given front-page treatment. No, I mean news as in something your reader hasn't heard before *and* that they will find useful for their job, hobby or life in general. It should also have the feel of a letter as opposed to an ad, brochure or press release.

4. It's delivered via email, in plain text or HTML, so you have the chance to link to your, or other, websites and use the full possibilities of the web.

5. It's sent to a group of people, which might tempt you to address them collectively (don't do it).

6. And they have asked you to send it to them, that is, they've opted in. Which means you have their permission to contact them, and something more important and very fragile: their trust.

> It should also have the feel of a letter as opposed to an ad, brochure or press release.

Great, I hear you say. So we just migrate our current newsletter to the web then. Er, no. Here's why. Old-school company newsletters are usually stuffed with photos of people receiving awards or grinning uneasily at a computer screen pretending to work. Typical articles focus on the company's acquisition of a new photocopier. Or perhaps an office move. Often, the bulk is taken up by thinly disguised plugs for new products. And who reads these slick epistles? I'll tell you. Nobody, that's who. Er, OK, some people do…

…the marketing manager. Those members of the Board who don't have enough to do that day. The proofreader (assuming they use one, which, to judge from the average issue, most don't). Here's who you won't find reading them. Customers. And do you know *why* they don't read them? Because they're *boring*.

Strengths

So why go to the (undoubted) time and trouble of publishing an e-zine? It's simple. Your subscribers are your best prospects. You have their permission to contact them regularly (could be weekly, or even daily). They will know, trust and respect you as a source of unbiased information on a subject that interests them.

In my line of work, as in most others, customers buy when they need my services, rather than when I want them to. That's why using direct mail, paradoxically given it's an area I specialise in, isn't so successful for me. My e-zine gives me a way to contact them 12 times a year and *remind* them that I exist.

Whatever your line of business, you have a product or service that people want. Now, they pay for that, which is only fair. But why not give them something for nothing? Information. Let's look at what your e-zine could be about. If you sell information, you're home and dry. Just repurpose a few snippets of editorial and you have a readymade e-zine. Sell garden equipment? Your e-zine could give people tips on gardening. If you are a conference organiser, give them highlights from recent events you've run.

Get your e-zine right and it acts as a source of highly qualified sales leads, orders, new clients, publicity and profits. If you are marketing a knowledge-based business like a small consultancy, you can use your e-zine to establish your reputation as an expert in your chosen field, whether that's business coaching or web design. In a product-based business, perhaps where you have aggressive competitors willing to trade on price, you can create some space between you and them by adding value for your customers with your e-zine.

It's not free to create, write, market and distribute an e-zine, but compared to the costs of media advertising or direct mail, it's a no-brainer. The simplest proof I can give you of this is that I use one and so do thousands of small businesses who would never dream of stumping up the tens of thousands of pounds (minimum) it would cost them to reach an international audience.

Written properly, and with effective policies for subscribing and, just as importantly, unsubscribing, you have a relationship-building tool that becomes self-sustaining, as subscribers forward it to their friends and colleagues.

Weaknesses

The e-zine's strength is also its weakness. Because it's emailed, it's subject to the vagaries of your subscribers' schedules, attention spans and willingness on any given day to open and read yet more words. Then there are spam filters, of which more in a moment. Think of your own inbox for a moment. You probably subscribe to at least one regular e-zine, maybe from a media site, a blog or a guru of one stripe of another. You know that they're interesting, but you also know they're not urgent. They aren't from your spouse, your boss or your best friend, so you can afford to leave them unread until you have time. Which may be never.

And because it's a soft communication, with little or no overt selling content, your e-zine won't make you a fortune. It has to work as part of a concerted marketing strategy that includes other channels more directly geared to sales.

What can you use it for?

You should think of your e-zine as one of the tools (perhaps your main tool) that you use to maintain relationships with your customers. Although the selling should be subtle, you can do it, in fact you should do it. You can use your e-zine to give:

- practical advice on using your product
- tips on doing the thing you do professionally (they may come to you for help)
- news of events where they can meet or learn from you
- pointers to interesting, relevant websites or blogs
- updates of new products or promotions

- checklists and questionnaires
- book reviews

…and to ask your subscribers to:

- Forward it to a friend
- Visit your website for more information about the topics covered
- Book places on training courses or seminars
- Come to a roadshow or product demonstration
- Check out pages on Amazon, eBay, YouTube, MySpace, Facebook, Twitter and the rest

What goes wrong

Boring

If your subscribers have signed up for your e-zine *My Imaginary Ailments*, then your weekly run-down of strange little spots between your knuckles and a vague sense of unease whenever you eat raisins will have them enthralled and emailing you with their own hypochondriacal moments. But if they signed up to Power Presenting the same catalogue of anxieties will have them unsubscribing in droves. So, what's boring depends on who's reading and what you promised them in the first place.

Even if you stick to the subject at hand, you'd better be able to write well and, if possible, entertainingly about it. Nobody likes being lectured, especially in an email, so simply unburdening yourself of all you know about bonsai, bike maintenance or balloon animal making without considering your reader will cost you subscribers.

Badly written

It may be emailed, but it's more, much more, than 'just an email'. You need to give your e-zine just as much attention as you do any other form of copywriting. If it's riddled with spelling mistakes, clunky with bad grammar, hobbled by poor punctuation or just plain ugly, you'll turn off your readers. It must be pleasurable to read, not merely informative. Remember, people are taking time out of their busy lives to read your e-zine, so make it enjoyable for them.

Impersonal

Relationships are built retail not wholesale. So if your e-zine feels and sounds like it's preaching to a crowd instead of chatting to one person, your subscribers won't feel the sense of connection they need to go on opening and reading your missives, week after week, month after month. Easiest way to do this (the bad thing, I mean)? Start your issue 'As some of you know…'

Overtly selling

You promised your subscribers practical advice or useful information, or news reviews, or a list of the funniest YouTube clips each week or…whatever. You didn't promise them, and they would never have opted in to receive, an unending stream of hysterical sales pitches. So don't treat your list as a captive audience. They're anything but captive, as your opt-out list will show you every time you go hard-sell on them. I'd suggest devoting no more than 25% of your e-zine to promotion, and even then, keep the copy a few ticks down on the salesometer.

Too short

You make a commitment when you start publishing an e-zine. Part of that commitment is to start acting like a publisher and delivering content your readers want. And you have to deliver it in sufficient quantity. Too much bite-sized information and you run the risk that there's not enough of 'you' in it to cement the bond you hope to form with your subscribers. Want an arbitrary figure? OK, your e-zine should be at least three screens' worth of material excluding all the opt-in/opt-out stuff.

> **I'd suggest devoting no more than 25% of your e-zine to promotion.**

Too long

Conversely, if your e-zine is too long, people will start feeling reading it's a chore. And nobody likes doing chores, right? The aim is to strike a balance. If your main article copy is more than 700 words you'd better be pretty sure you're telling an irresistible story.

What you must include

You should definitely include useful information in your e-zine. In a moment I'll give you some ideas for what you could write about. You should also include some low-level sales messages. Maybe a few house ads promoting your products or services. Or offering downloads such as white papers and checklists from your website.

I'd also strive to develop a personal feel to your e-zine, which means including enough information about yourself to make your subscribers feel they have a relationship with either you personally, your organisation or your brand. It's my view that, for all that companies and their advertising agencies talk about the primacy of brands and the relationships customers have with the brand, most people tend to prefer relationships with other people.

Your e-zine is personal to you and your organisation. That will determine the precise content. But here's a checklist of all the important housekeeping stuff as well as some ideas for articles:

Housekeeping
At the top…
- A branding device: either a logo or a masthead – to give your e-zine an identity
- The e-zine's name – try to be a little more creative than calling it XYZ Company News. If you sell fishing tackle, you could call it, 'Reel 'Em In!'
- A slogan or strapline that tells subscribers what it's about. So our fishing tackle e-zine could say, 'Helping you catch prize-winning fish'.
- Details of the e-zine itself and the issue:

- Photo and name of the 'publisher' – that's you.
- Publication date, e.g. March 2009.
- Volume and issue number e.g. Volume 10, number 3 for the March edition of an e-zine in its tenth year.
- How often you publish.
- ISSN (that's international standard serial number). I applied for mine from the British Library. Not compulsory but adds a touch of authority to your e-zine.
- Succinct information on how to manage your subscription (a euphemism for unsubscribing) and how to subscribe (because the reader may have had it forwarded to them).
- You could also include a brief table of contents if you have more than one article or item in your e-zine.

At the bottom...

- Your privacy policy. It doesn't have to be long, but it does have to be clear. Something to the effect that you don't pass on, swap or rent out subscriber email addresses.
- A copyright notice – because for everything you write you automatically own the copyright, like this © Andy Maslen, 2009.
- A street address for the publisher. If you are home-based, I strongly advise you to get a PO box. That way you can protect your own privacy.
- Your phone number, email address and web address/es.
- Explicit instructions on how to unsubscribe.

Ideas for articles

You may find that writing about the subject you love comes naturally and you can generate ideas for a dozen articles at a time, or whenever you need one. For the times when you need a little inspiration, here are five thematic ideas that I've always found work for me

Practical advice

The 'How to' article is a sure-fire winner because your subscribers will always want to gain insider knowledge. It's also good because the headline practically writes itself. It's going to start with the words, 'How to…'. So you could have…

- How to invest like a hedge fund manager
- How to run your car on water
- How to triple your income overnight
- How to write better e-zine articles
- How to jump higher
- How to make your household budget go further

You get the picture, I'm sure.

Top tips

Done as a list this is pretty easy article to write. You pick your topic then come up with a headline that says something like…

15 insider secrets of effective houseboat building

Ten ways management in 2010 will be different

23 routes to copywriting success

Case study

Take a recent client assignment that went well and write it up. Keep it briefer than a full-blown case study (which you can find out how to write in Chapter 3).

Fireside chat

Why not interview a colleague, client or contact who has particular expertise or a great story to tell. People love reading interviews and it lends itself to the concise form of an e-zine. Just be sure to follow the simple Q&A approach you see in magazines.

Research

If you or your company has done some research, you can take a few snippets or headline findings and condense them into an e-zine article. Or spend some time on the net and dig up examples of credible or even controversial research you can comment on. Remember to keep it relevant to your e-zine and, more importantly, your subscribers.

What you can leave out

The high-level answer to the question, 'What should I leave out of my e-zine?' is twofold:

• Stuff that bores your subscribers.
• Stuff that triggers spam filters.

The second is slightly more complex. We should probably say, 'stuff that triggers automated spam filters or is sufficiently annoying and/or offensive that your subscribers label it as spam.'
  I'd say omit all of the following:

• Extended corporate profiles (nobody cares).
• Detailed product descriptions (unless your e-zine is explicitly cast as a product catalogue – in which case it's not really an e-zine at all).
• Ads for products and services you haven't thoroughly vetted (because your subscribers trust you and your recommendations and will not take kindly to you shilling for snake-oil salesmen).

How to structure it

Structure your e-zine in five zones and you won't go far wrong. Here's how I do it.

Zone1: Masthead and publication details

This is where you establish your brand and define the look and feel of your e-zine. Are you going to be fun, entertaining, brash, sophisticated, professional, easygoing, chatty, formal (please no), authoritative, playful? You and your designer can create that image through the name of your e-zine and the logo or graphics you use.

Zone 2: A note from the publisher

This is where you really establish the personality of your e-zine. If you are self-employed or any kind of one-man or woman band then it's your chance to inject your own personality into the e-zine. That, after all, is what your clients are ultimately buying. You can write a short letter using a personalised opening – Dear Jo – and a friendly sign off with a signature graphic. Don't get too personal: your subscribers don't (or shouldn't) want to know what you had for breakfast or the colour and size of that embarrassing little whatsit on your doodah. Just enough to show them you are more than a wizard car detailer, knitting pattern designer, investment guru or model aircraft engineer.

Zone 3: The main article/s

Here's your chance to shine. This is what your subscribers bought into. A weekly or monthly dose of your wisdom on the subject you're an expert on. You must deliver here or you will go nowhere. Do your research, be opinionated, give them facts, advise them: in short, write interesting stuff they can't get from anyone else.

Zone 4: Ads

Whether they're selling your stuff or stuff for affiliates or contacts in your network, there's nothing wrong with including a few discreet ads in your e-zine. Find a way to mark them off so readers know what they are (and can choose to ignore them if they want). Using hypertext in the main article or the letter from the publisher is an excellent way to link to more detailed promotional copy on your website.

Zone 5: Housekeeping information

State your privacy policy at the bottom, where it can be clearly seen but where it doesn't interfere with the main body of your e-zine. Explain how to unsubscribe and give a clear link. Don't make people reply with Unsubscribe in the subject line – just give them a one-click link to an automated unsubscribe page.

Notes on style and tone of voice

The main style point to remember when you're writing an e-zine is that because it's coming into your subscribers' inboxes, they're going to lump it in with all email. That means it's contributing to their overall stress levels as yet another email to be dealt with. And, yes, I know they opted in, but they may have done that on a day and at a time when they were feeling laid back. Or maybe they just wanted the freebie you used to entice them to sign up.

So, keep your writing tight, keep it conversational and keep it (reasonably) brief. A little tip I have found useful is to give them a word count at the top and indicate roughly how long it will take to read that particular issue.

Remember, also, that the e-zine truly comes into its own as a publicity vehicle for solo professionals (though it can work extremely well for companies too). So try to give your e-zine a personal flavour and make it feel like it's your authentic voice. Avoid business-speak or jargon – unless that's what your subscribers are looking for.

> **Keep your writing tight, keep it conversational and keep it (reasonably) brief.**

My five top tips for e-zine copy

1. Keep your tone of voice informal but authoritative
Nobody wants a lecture. And they don't want advertising puff, either. You have to know your stuff and you need to communicate it as if you mean it.

2. Keep your style tight and use plain English
Remember your medium is email. People feel busier than normal when they are reading their emails. So make it easy to understand. Use simple words and short sentences. Break up your e-zine into short paragraphs and use section-heads to help your reader navigate quickly to the stuff that interests them.

3. Think hard about your subject line

Once again, it's all that stands between your e-zine and the trash. Namecheck your e-zine and try to give a flavour of the content, too. And, for email clients like Outlook that allow readers to see the email before opening it, your first six or seven lines are crucial since they act as a sneak preview of your content.

4. Make sure you give practical information

Ultimately, this is a resource for your readers. They want something they can use in their work or personal lives. So provide tips, tools and techniques. How to beat greenfly on competition roses. How to win the war for talent. How to stay well-informed about the web.

5. Remember to sell

Make sure you don't get so wrapped up in the journalism that you forget to sell. It doesn't have to be a hard sell. This is in any case counterproductive. Instead, remind people that you have products for sale that will help them even further to enjoy or benefit from this particular aspect of their lives.

Using images

Images can work well in e-zines. But remember that not everyone can see them in their email clients. Make sure your e-zine works without them, so don't have articles that don't make sense without the images. It's probably best to use them sparingly as the masthead and maybe as navigation devices or ways of breaking up the e-zine into more manageable chunks. A photo of the publisher – you – is an instant way to literally establish a face for the e-zine and to give it a personality. It also humanises it, placing it above most of the soulless blast emails amongst which it sits in the inbox.

Andy Maslen, Publisher

February 2009
Vol. 9 No.2
ISSN 1752-0177
Published every month.
To manage your
subscription, see the end
of this message.
Sign me up for this ezine.

In this issue:

- Main article:**How to beat writer's block** [556 words, around four minutes to read]
- Your teacher would be so proud: tips on better English
- What I'm reading
- Quote of the month

....

Hi Karen,

Cool. Snow!

As I write this, there's thick snow outside my office window. (In fact, sshh, don't tell, I skived off for an hour yesterday to build a snowman with my kids.)

I also got involved in a giant snowball fight involving kids AND parents on the way home from school. There's a lovely lesson for us copywriters in all of this...

Sometimes all it takes is a little trigger to unlock people's inner motivations. That trigger could be a few tons of frozen water plopping down onto the ground. Or your copy.

If you want to work on your ability to tap into people's motivations, there are still a few places left on our first ever open copywriting training course. It's on 28 April in Central London and you can get all the details by clicking here.

Our other business news is that Jo Maslen, our Commercial Director, is now consulting to clients who need help getting brand and marketing messages across to customer-facing staff. Find out more about Jo's services and background by clicking here.

Till next month,

Andy

Figure 8 The opening screen from the author's monthly e-zine Maslen on Marketing

Every month, as well as the main article, I open with a more personal update about what I've been doing – putting the 'news' in newsletter. This is where I give the e-zine some personality. It's also where I insert most of the links.

By putting all the important stuff including a list of contents up top, I let subscribers check it out in their reading pane before opening.

CHAPTER 9
CORPORATE BROCHURE

IN 1847, OUR FOUNDER, JOSIAH SNODGRASS...Zzzz

Introduction

Hear that ringing sound? It's the sales rep from your printer hammering the sales bell off its bracket. You've just given them the job of printing your corporate brochure. With all the colour photos, waxed end-paper, spot varnish and die cutting, corporate brochures have kept many a firm of printers in the black. But what is it about corporate brochures that makes them both hideously expensive to produce and virtually unreadable?

I suspect the culprit is our old friend hubris. In ancient Greece, hubris was the worst crime imaginable – desecrating your enemy's corpse to inflict humiliation and boost your own image. Nowadays it's come to mean any act or behaviour stemming from overbearing pride or arrogance. Now, it may be a stretch to get from classical Athens to the average 24-page A4 glossy piece of corporate puff. But the fact remains, most corporate brochures say more about the company's opinion of itself than anything else. And guess what. That opinion is usually – or at least if you believe what you're reading – extremely proud. And, therefore, extremely BORING.

Don't get me wrong, your business may have discovered a drug that cures cancer. You may have a team of people so accomplished at what they do that they are sought out as advisers to governments. Your products may contribute to the wellbeing of whole societies, relieving gun crime, voter apathy or racial prejudice. It's just that the dreaded corporate brochure seems to exist in a special world, where everyone involved in its creation has forgotten a simple truth.

People aren't interested in what you think of yourself.

People are interested in *themselves*. It's why the best direct mail letters speak directly to the reader – about their hopes and fears…their motivations and reservations… their deepest desires and secret feelings.

And guess how many people actually read them? Corporate brochures, I mean. Well, some, I suppose, if we're being charitable. But how many then go on to behave differently towards the company that issued them? I'd say none. Why is this? It turns out that wading through page after page of the usual hubristic business-speak leaves your average punter looking for some drying paint to watch as light relief. But it doesn't have to be like this.

Corporate brochures can serve an important purpose other than demonstrating a company's overweening pride in its own achievements. To do so they must focus on the reader, just like a good direct mail letter. Given where most end up, it's humbling to think how much money gets spent creating matt-laminated, art-directed, foil-blocked, full-colour bin liners.

Strengths

Clearly, any business with the resources to produce a corporate brochure is not on its uppers. (Though they may be shortly after paying the print bill.) So they're a great way of signalling to clients, employees and creditors that you are a force to be reckoned with – financially strong and with a story to tell. Your sales team will love giving them out and feel they have an edge. So they're more motivated, which is definitely a good thing.

In the absence of newspapers, trade magazines or a TV in your reception area, visitors will idly flick through them and may pick up a few salient points about how doing business with you is good for them. That's good too. They are also tangible. Websites have displaced corporate brochures as the principal repository of corporate self-promotion, yet they lack the permanence and touchability of brochures.

Done right, the corporate brochure is your best shot at giving someone a broad view of what you're all about. Your values, the sort of business you are to work with (and for) your strengths, your complete product range, and the views of your clients, maybe with some engaging stories about how you've helped them. The crucial phrase is, 'done right'. Which is what this chapter is all about.

> They must focus on the reader, just like a good direct mail letter.

Weaknesses

Here's what I think happens when a company embarks on a corporate brochure. First comes the rationale. This varies, but could be:

- 'We've had a great year – let's tell everyone about how great we are.'
- 'Our parent company has forgotten we exist.'
- 'I saw a brochure our competitors put out with *their* CEO on page 1.'
- 'Investors are losing confidence in us.'
- 'If we don't use up our corporate marketing budget, we won't get it next year.'
- 'Our sales guys say they need a corporate brochure.'

Next, a protracted series of meetings involving lots of board directors who should be busy running the company, where they toss around concepts like 'key messages' and photo shoot locations. Finally, a team of writers, photographers, designers and printers (let's not forget the printers – they'd be feeding their families on scraps for half the year if it weren't for corporate brochures) is assembled, briefed and set to work.

Roughly six months later (it takes this long because the CEO, having ignored the detailed running of the communications department for much of the year, suddenly discovers a long-held affinity for editing and art direction), the brochure is unveiled to much tarantara and champagne (the vintage and quality of which determined largely by whatever's left after the brochure has been printed). Clients receive them in the post. Exhibition visitors have them thrust hotly into their unwilling hands. Investors and journalists get them in goody bags at swanky receptions. And then what? Usually, they get stuck on a shelf or pushed to the back of a drawer along with all the others. That was certainly my experience as both recipient and donor of corporate brochures.

The problem is nobody really knows what they're supposed to do with a corporate brochure. Not the marketing department who created it, not the sales team who asked for it, and unfortunately, but not surprisingly, not the client who's given it.

What can you use it for

This is a tricky one. I could give you a facetious answer about loft insulation and righting wobbly office furniture but then you'd feel short-changed. So, you can use corporate brochures for the following:

- Repositioning your business if you've just acquired it or embarked on a new corporate strategy.
- Gaining investor confidence (and therefore funding).
- Reassuring potential customers that you are big enough to be an effective supplier or partner.
- Showing existing customers the full range of things you could do for them.
- Giving potential employees the corporate story (though you may want a special employee-focused version).
- Impressing journalists who attend press launches.
- Influencing policymakers (politicians, civil servants, legislators, regulators).

Not a bad list of fairly serious objectives for a few sheets of paper, I think you'll agree.

What goes wrong

Ah yes, what goes wrong. Here's a short but non-exhaustive list:

'Corporate' copywriting

Even companies who send out perfectly good direct mail or e-shots – personalised and personal, written in plain English and as punchy as a boxer on steroids – can come over all unnecessary when it comes to writing the corporate brochure. The rules become never say in one word what you can say in five. Never use a short word when a longer one is available. And never make any bleeding sense if you can possibly avoid it. I suspect it has something to do with the involvement of that rarely seen but influential body of people – the Board. (I sometimes wonder whether the Board are just 'the bored', which would explain why they are so ready to get involved in corporate brochures.)

'Oh no, that won't do,' they intone, when the copywriter offers a lucid sentence in plain English, perhaps explaining that the company manufactures drill bits for mining equipment. 'We think it would sound better if you talked about 'best-of-breed, geomorphological intervention solutions'.'

Ostentation

The very first corporate brochure I was ever involved in producing was hideously expensive. About £10 a pop, if memory serves. This was in the late 1980s. Why? Well, we could start with the illustrator we hired to paint a dozen or so pictures. Then there was the cover paper, woven from chinchilla hair, or antique Persian rug offcuts, or lily stamens. Finally, the non-standard size – a good idea in some ways, but it meant we had to send them in Tyvek envelopes – an additional cost. We managed to avoid foil blocking, spot varnish and all the other showy devices that cause printers to start browsing the Mercedes website, but only just.

Library shots

It's funny how often organisations who gladly inform the reader of their 20,000 employees worldwide feel that none of them are valuable enough to be photographed for the corporate brochure. Instead we are treated to the usual suspects: the pretty girls, hunky boys and silver-haired though clearly still up for an hour of squash at 7.00 am male executives. People point at laptops and smile enigmatically, shake hands, sit around in conference rooms being creative (you can tell they're being creative because there are coffee mugs on the table and they're wearing T-shirts and jumpers instead of suits).

Or maybe there's a stack of smooth flat pebbles... or an Emperor Penguin... or a watch spring. Why? Who knows.

Committee effects

The corporate brochure is the ultimate committee-driven creative project. It's too important for one person to be in charge. Usually the communications manager is given the responsibility for producing it, but to call her 'in charge' is to completely misunderstand the brief. She is there to assemble a team that will include any or all of the following: copywriter, designer, photographer, illustrator and printer; and to liaise with all the departmental or regional barons who will need to be consulted about the content. And to show drafts/proofs to those who will, eventually, sign it off. On projects I have worked on, this latter group has included, variously, regional managing directors, regional presidents, divisional managing directors, marketing directors, brand directors and global CEOs.

The result is often a brochure that, rather than following the unified 'vision' so proudly advertised within its pages, is, instead, the version hated by the fewest members of the committee.

No purpose

The corporate brochure is beautiful. It is sleek. It is impressive. The recipients have no idea why you have given it to them. Too often, in all the brouhaha surrounding their production, one crucial question is overlooked (or never asked): 'What do we hope to gain by doing this?'. 'Or, to be more precise, 'What do we want people to do once they have finished reading this brochure?'. Every other marketing expenditure is supposed to have some sort of measurable ROI, except this one. But why? In print terms it's one of the most expensive items on the budget.

A mild desire (and request) to have people call to discuss becoming a customer would be an entirely suitable and not-out-of-keeping goal for any corporate brochure.

What you must include

When you're writing
a corporate brochure,
remember you need
to have a commercial
goal. Producing
something merely
eye-catching isn't
enough.

When you're writing a corporate brochure, start with a plan. At the top of your plan you have a line that explains why you're producing it. It will have some sort of commercial rationale. You must include all the facts, stories and information you need to achieve that goal. For example, if one of the purposes of the brochure is to convince investors to take part in an initial public offering (IPO), make sure you explain how solid the company's future is and provide evidence for the claims you're making for future profitability.

On the other hand, if you want to convince people you are not a rapacious monster, exploiting your staff and the world generally for profit, a nice section on corporate social responsibility (CSR) might go down well.

Think about the following:

- A letter from your president, CEO or chairman.
- Photos of staff (not just senior people, have a few forklift drivers or retail assistants as well).
- Testimonials from customers (preferably with their photos too).
- Case studies.
- Discussion of how you help your clients meet the typical challenges facing them.
- A profile of your organisation.
- High level product information.
- Press cuttings.
- Details of your good works (see CSR above).
- Contact details.

What you can leave out

Can you sense a smile of self-satisfaction stealing across your CEO's face as she reads the first proofs? Leave out the stuff making her smile. It's not for her. Or you. Or the communications director. It's for the reader: employee, customer, journalist, investor. You don't, really, even want to make *them* smile. What you want is for them to know, feel and commit to the things you want them to. Although corporate brochures often look like art, they aren't art, and their creators shouldn't be concerned with the same reactions as artists. So, leave out these:

Empty adjectives

I've listed a few of these in Chapter 12 (and in other writing on copywriting). Adjectives are there to add information, not emphasis, so those to look out for include major, significant, revolutionary, ground-breaking, best-of-breed and, of course, exciting.

Fad words

'Our people are united in their passionate drive for excellence.' Or is that, 'Our people are driven by a united passion for excellence.' Or 'Our excellent people are passionately driven to excel.' This sort of phrasemaking is spawned by the business world's ever-present hunger for new ways of disguising some fairly ordinary sentiments.

A brief tour round the workplaces of many of these passion-driven organisations would reveal the truth: a workforce ground down by long hours, stress and lack of direction. And customers know this: every time they pick up the phone or make face-to-face contact, they can tell what unites a company's employees. If it doesn't fit with the copy in the corporate brochure, they don't say, 'Oh well, must have been an off-day,' they say, 'Huh! More corporate hype.'

If your employees are passionate about their work, a) it will show and b) you can get them to tell their own stories (with a little help from your copywriter).

Over-detailed product information

I have seen this happen where members of the committee who will approve the brochure have product or service-line responsibility. And, to be fair to them, you can't expect the head of product marketing not to fight for as much product information to be included as possible. But a corporate brochure is not the place to give – much less read – page after page of bullet points and long copy extolling the features, advantages and benefits of your entire product range.

The entire history of your organisation

Are your customers interested in the history of your business since its foundation above a fish and chip shop in East London in 1932? If they are, great! You can give them a timeline, a commentary, an essay on changing social conditions and economic development from the early Thirties to the present day. But…

If you suspect that the only people who really care about your rise from humble beginnings to global supremacy are your Board, your founder or your owner, you must argue for a trimmed down version. Keep the timeline if you must, keep a few milestones, but focus on the *present*. Your customers are dealing with you *now*.

As much 'we' as possible

I know it's difficult. After all, this is about you. But your reader just isn't that interested: they'd much rather read about themselves, or at least how you are going to solve their problems. So try swapping as many 'we's as you can for 'you'. You'll end up with copy that's far more readable and far more likely to engage your reader.

How to structure it

Begin by thinking about your reader. Once they have finished reading your brochure, what would you like them to know, feel and commit to? Do you want them to feel excited about doing business with you? Reassured that their money is in safe hands? Do you want them to pick up the phone and arrange a sales meeting? Send you a cheque for fifty thousand dollars? Apply for a job? Drop that investigation under Sarbanes-Oxley? It's all possible. *But only if you begin with your reader, not yourself.*

So be creative with the format. A bit creative might mean a square brochure. Very creative might mean ditching the brochure altogether and producing some completely new format. A food package. Or a toy box. A toolkit. Or an artist's easel. I wrote a corporate brochure for one client that was destined to end up as a board game, complete with box, playing surface, card decks and rules.

But we're getting ahead of ourselves. Before you start ordering brass nuts and bolts instead of staples, or sheets of gold leaf, we need to plan our copy. As with all the pieces discussed in this book, there's no hard and fast rule about what goes where in a corporate brochure, but here's a suggested format that should get you going, one I've used successfully for a number of clients. It's something akin to a website site plan. Even if you end up rearranging the individual sections, these are the big themes I think every corporate brochure should cover:

Introduction – could be in the form of a letter from your top bod, or maybe a quirky one from a less senior employee or a technical specialist like an engineer or a nurse. In it, I'd set the scene for the rest of the brochure partly by explaining what you hope the reader will get out of reading and partly by alluding to the overall social, environmental, economic, business or political climate you're operating in.

Who we are – this is the About Us page. It could include sub-sections that talk about your business philosophy, your people, your mission, vision or values, your history and development. You could give statistics and data that show your size in financial and human terms, your growth over a particular period and your assets, especially if they're interesting ones, like the number of patents you hold, your R&D investment or the square miles of forests you manage sustainably (you probably need to if you're printing a corporate brochure).

What we do – provide an *overview of* your products and services. Remember to keep this section tight, top-level and focused on the characteristics that unify them, such as the way you only develop a new product if you believe it can make a real difference to clients' profitability, or their carbon-neutral footprint.

What makes us special – whether you operate in a commodity market or not – and the Internet makes all of us commodity suppliers to a degree – you have to work hard to show your reader how you differ from your competitors. Do you have an in-house training academy? Have you invented a web-based technology that makes your way of doing things faster, better and cheaper? Are all your employees psychic? Find out, and write it down.

Customer stories – switch viewpoints to that of your reader and tell stories from customers. Case studies in other words. Use pictures if you can to bring the stories to life and give the reader a break from all that copy. Remember to structure your case studies in a logical and coherent sequence – see Chapter 3 for how to do it. Try to cross-reference the case studies to your special skills so they reinforce the previous section.

Call to action – yes, your corporate brochure needs a call to action. Why not, after spending all that money, get some measurable ROI? Tell them how to get in touch and even incentivise them in some way. You could offer a white paper, free consultation or audit of some kind.

Notes on style and tone of voice

OK, first of all? Try to stay down to earth. Most corporate brochures go hurtling into the sky tethered to a huge gasbag filled with hot air. They usually sound like a cross between a lawyer out of a Charles Dickens novel and a futuristic technocrat. In sentences like this one:

> Indeed it can be said that XYZ Corporation has delivered consistently superior service through the delivery of client-centric best practice solutions and proprietary web-based synergy applications.

There's no reason why your corporate brochure should sound like a pompous old fart. Instead, why not reach out to your reader with the same style you (or your direct marketing department) would employ in a mailshot. After all, it's the same people reading it.

That means using plain English. And *that* means…

- Short words rather than longer synonyms.
- Short sentences – aim for around 16 words on average.
- A preference for Anglo Saxon over Latin- and Greek-derived words (let instead of permit, stop instead of terminate and before instead of prior to).
- No jargon – so 'solutions' is banned.

In terms of tone of voice, aim for a conversational tone. OK, it can be slightly more formal than a mailshot or press ad if you really feel you need to come across all serious and authoritative. But remember that most people, even senior executive types, are bored rigid by this stiff, self-congratulatory copywriting.

Using images

Remember that for many people, photographs of your directors or office block are of limited interest, however beautifully they're lit, however artfully they're composed. So, for that matter, are abstract or high-art concepts, unrelated pictures of wildlife and the whole panoply of stock images – especially those involving models in business attire or hard hats whom you pretend work for your company.

I was once commissioned by a firm of large-format printers to produce a corporate brochure for them. The concept was called The Print Buyer's Guide. It consisted of two slip-cased A5 ring binders, one with loose-leaf sheets giving information on everything from litho printing to the dimensions for bus-side advertising, the other a selection of the different stocks they could print on.

The image our photographer shot for the front cover was inspired: a close-up of four huge tins of ink: cyan, magenta, yellow and black. They weren't pristine – each one had drips and runs from the rim to the base. But they perfectly captured the business of printing in a way I had never seen before – and haven't since.

Original photography like this has many advantages over stock shots. You own the copyright – or you do if you make sure the photographer assigns it to you. At the very least, you have an exclusive licence to use it, so you won't open your morning paper and find another company using the same image currently gracing the front cover of *your* brochure. You can use it to tell a story that's personal to your organisation. If you feature your own employees, you get some free motivation from your staff, who will be pleasantly surprised to be chosen – and rewarded – in this way.

You could consider taking photographs of your customers – there's no better way I can think of to prove your are a customer-centric organisation than to depict them in your corporate brochure. Again, as with your staff, most clients will be flattered to be asked.

As an aside, while I was writing this section an executive search firm (posh recruitment agency) emailed me a PDF corporate brochure. Here, in sequence are the images they use to illustrate it: a shiny office block, the insides of a clock, a computer keyboard, a compass, two men grinning inanely while shaking hands, a page of stock prices with a clear glass marble resting on it, a page of stock prices without a clear glass marble resting on it, three separate photographs of people speaking into mobile phones, an hourglass, an attractive man and an attractive woman gazing at some paper, another keyboard and three-interlocking jigsaw pieces. Court adjourned for sentencing and psychiatric reports.

A word on design

Perhaps because most organisations tend to consult a designer rather than a copywriter when they're thinking about producing a corporate brochure, most are design-led. Copy tends to be slotted in afterwards – sometimes it would seem almost an afterthought – made to fit whatever slice of real estate the designers have left among the white space, Amazonian tree frogs and Leonardo-Da-Vinci-a-like diagrams.

I have a wonderful example in my Black Museum, where every alternate page has the copy white reversed out of pale grey. Leaving aside the somewhat, shall we say, challenging point size, this typographical mannerism renders the copy virtually unreadable. Hey ho – the pictures look nice.

Instead of this approach, here is my recommendation:

Either start with the copy and then ask your designer to make it attractive and readable or ask your designer to arrange for you to meet the copywriter they intend to use at the start of the project. Make sure everyone understands what the communications goals of the brochure are and that having people be able to read the copy is crucial to achieving them. *If* the designer then comes back with grey type on a dark blue ground, ask them how easy this will be to read compared to black on white or dark grey on cream.

Figure 9 Corporate brochure for Lewis Direct Mail, a business-to-business direct mail company

For this corporate brochure, we majored on benefits copy – just like a direct mail letter. We used simple techniques like dark type on a white background so people could read it, and original photography of the employees doing what they do best.

A track record you can rely on

We opened our doors for business in 1966: a two-room operation in Victoria. Since then, we have grown year-by-year, and now occupy a greatly expanded site in central London comprising four buildings of 20,000 sq ft.

In the intervening years, we have handled over 50,000 mailings – more than 100 million individual envelopes mailed to 195 countries. We specialise in small to medium-sized mailings: from as few as 50 to 100,000 or more.

In a typical week at Lewis, w[...] and despatch, you never hav[...] than a day.

Keeping pace with [...]

From a simple lettershop bus[...] sophistication of the direct m[...] But our guiding principles re[...] to your deadlines, at the best[...]

Some of our clients have bee[...] with us for ten years or more[...] the job. To provide detailed f[...] initiative, identifying obstacle[...] quickly with suggestions for [...]

Our team:
an extension of your marketing department –

We believe the success of our business depends not just on the calibre of the people we employ, but also the relationships we develop with our clients. These relationships are particularly valuable at those all-too-familiar moments when everyone in your team seems to have arrived within the last six months.

– providing the continuity that keeps your business running smoothly

Staff turnover in marketing departments is a fact of life. But our detailed knowledge of our clients' direct mail operations means we can provide continuity, ensuring a smooth flow of mailings and providing new members of your team with advice and guidance while they find their feet.

We employ more than 50 people in six departments: account management, data processing, laser printing, lettershop, warehouse and despatch, and overseas consolidation. Our departmental managers work together to ensure a smooth workflow for all your mailings.

Your Account Manager:
a single point of contact at all times

And to keep you in the picture, we assign you a dedicated Account Manager. This gives you a single point of contact – no merry-go-round of different people to get an answer – and a representative at Lewis. Your Account Manager ensures that your mailings are booked in and run smoothly to your instructions, right up to despatch.

To further streamline your mailings, and eliminate uncertainty, we even assign individual data processing executives to your account, who can then become familiar with your data and style of list selections.

'We've been working with Lewis for over 20 years – they're more like an extra part of our marketing department than a separate company. Having a single point of contact – our Account Manager – makes life simple: I know that whatever I want, she's on hand to provide it.'

David Gudgin
Marketing Manager
Euromonitor

The point of the brochure was to emphasise the deep-level benefit of working with Lewis Direct Mail – that for busy multi-tasking marketing managers, this is a firm that allows you to relax, knowing they are covering all the bases. As a former client-turned copywriter, I knew this was true.

CHAPTER 10
EMAIL

**PLEASE DON'T
DELETE ME**

Introduction

This chapter is about promotional emails, which, for the most part, means HTML. This is a huge and ultra-fast evolving subject. That means two things for you and me. One, I don't have the space to go into all the details of email *marketing*, from click-through rate optimization to best day of the week to mail metrics so I'm going to stick to email *copywriting*. That is the premise of this book, after all. Two, by the time it's published, much of what I write about the best way to use email may have been superseded. Again, by sticking to the principles of copywriting for email, I hope to avoid that fate as much as I can. This is still a field in its infancy and shows no sign of settling into a predictable pattern. The best advice I can give you is to find out what works for you and your business and stick to that, whilst, of course, testing rigorously and continuously.

For the inside scoop on what's working and what's not, try *MarketingSherpa* www.marketingsherpa.com or MailerMailer www.mailermailer.com.

A short word on personal emails

Although I could, I'm not going to go into a long piece about how to write business emails. That's one-to-one emails between you and your colleagues and contacts. Oh, OK then, just quickly. A few thoughts…

1 Always be polite. Good manners cost nothing, as they say. You can type Dear Fred in about a second if you practice. It takes about as long to type Best regards, Andy, or a fraction of that if you set up a little macro.

2 Check your spelling. But if you're really so super-busy and important that you feel you don't have to, at the very least, check you have spelled your recipient's name right. They'll forgive almost anything else but not that. See 1 above.

3 Get to the point, but be friendly too. You can give bad news or demand better payment terms without coming over as Attila the Hun.

4 If you're asking for action, give them a deadline. You'd be surprised how many people will respond if you tell them when you need their answer by.

5 Think hard about the impact your words will have on your reader. A 'funny' remark or word can sound offhand, sarcastic or rude at the other end. See 1 above.

Selling on screen

So, back to the true subject of this section, which is sales emails. Or, if you prefer, promotional emails. We're writing to sell. That might mean getting leads or orders, but we're looking for a change in behaviour that's going to benefit us and our business commercially.

Here are a few of the challenges we face when writing emails. First of all, your recipient can get rid of this intrusion into her working day without lifting a finger. Oh, OK, she does have to lift a finger, but only by four millimetres, before placing it back down on the mouse button to trash your promo. All she needs to do is check out your From field and subject line before deciding that, yep, this is junk mail. (Let's just hope she doesn't consider it the s-word and permanently block emails from you.) If she uses a preview pane, boy have you got a hurdle to jump. As she pages down through her emails, she can see a big chunk of yours without opening it.

Does it look interesting or boring? Relevant or time-wasting? How long have you got to persuade her? Current estimates say less than a second. Once your email is opened, it has to perform as well as the best sales letter and then some. We all know how flighty readers of promotional emails are – that's because we're those people too. A poor opening, an over-long sentence, lack of navigation or scannable elements will all encourage your reader to say goodbye.

Strengths

As with e-zines, one of the chief strengths of email as a promotional channel is that it's comparatively cheap... to send. You don't have to pay for printing, or envelopes or enclosing or stamps. You do have to pay for copy and design, deployment and tracking though. Or do it in house, which is hardly cost-free. But, yes, hit for hit, email is cheaper than snail mail.

You can also hit a huge number of people at more or less the same time and you have far greater control of the timing of delivery than you do with the post. If you want, you can send multiple messages to the same person on the same day. Try doing that the traditional way.

You can, if you want to, include animation or links to movie clips, web pages and blogs. And you have unlimited space. This depends on your subscribing to the school of thought that emails don't have to be short, but if you do, then you have a lot of space to play with.

Weaknesses

There are one or two. Let's start with the most obvious one. Spam filters. These fall into two categories: automated and human. Automated spam filters are designed to detect spam and trash it without the recipient having to do anything. But what is spam? Any promotional email? Or only those promising body part enlargement, instant riches or herbal health supplements? The general rule seems to be that if you aren't a spammer and you don't write or behave like one, you won't get into trouble. There are various free and paid-for resources on the web you can use to check your email copy before you send it.

The human spam filter is a little different. This is just the feeling you get when you've been sent a promotion that you feel is so irrelevant to you and your needs that you mark it as spam in the hope the next one won't reach you. This is more about targeting than copy, so be aware that however genuine you and your product are, if you are mailing men with a promotion for designer maternity wear, you'll get nowhere fast. (But then, that was always true.)

If you're in business-to-business (b2b) markets, you'll know that business people also feel busy and stressed when checking their emails. The nightmare scenario is coming back from a two-week break to find several thousand emails in your inbox. People have always felt busy, even in the days when everything was direct mail, but the phenomenal success of email has led to a whole industry of inbox-management training courses, advice sheets and internal drives to cut email traffic (I was even involved in writing copy for such a campaign for a large UK manufacturer). So there's a feeling that email is, of itself, a problem. Clearly, your promotional copy is going to have to sparkle to get past all that inertia and negative emotion.

It's also harder to read onscreen, though as screen resolutions improve and a generation of screen-based readers reaches maturity, I foresee this becoming less of a problem. But for now, it pays to ensure your designer sets the copy in a sufficiently large point size for people to read without eye strain. (Again, this was also true in the old days of print.)

What can you use it for

You can use email for exactly the same range of goals as you can sales letters. To recap:

- Generate enquiries.
- Push people to your website to get a download.
- Get requests for a white paper or free report.
- Generate requests for free samples or trial issues.
- Generate requests for a free product or service trial.
- Sell additional products or services to existing customers.
- Sell upgraded memberships.
- Ask for help finding new members – 'member-get-member'.
- Ask for awards nominees.

- Ask for speakers at a conference or seminar.
- Ask for feedback on a soft launch of a new website.

Give your reader an instant reason to keep reading.

In my experience, response rates are much higher for opted-in lists, which is not really surprising. Because it's a digital channel, email is particularly well suited to campaigns where you want to integrate the sales message with a website, either because you are asking for sign-ups or registrations, or because you want to demo a new technology or give people a download.

I have heard it said that you can't sell directly with an email. That they're best used for lead generation. This might be true for the people who have told me this, though they usually utter it as a universal truth. But I have one very good client who sold £1,000,000 worth of business reports from a single campaign using copy he wrote himself and delivered via email. As an attachment.

What goes wrong

Weak opening

Give your reader an instant reason to keep reading. What is the huge wow-factor difference your product can make to your reader's life? Give them that. Straight away. Emails that start off slow, with references to the state of play in the reader's industry, will almost certainly fail to engage. Why? Duh! Because they already *know* that.

Let's suppose you're selling an athletics training programme based on new scientific research. Your email could start like this…

Dear Fred,

Want to know the secret training breakthrough the US Olympic team is keeping to itself?

Not enough calls to action

Don't save your call to action to the end like a traditional direct mail letter. Bung one in immediately. At the top. Above the fold. And use a mixture of graphic and text links. Not everyone has their email client or browser set to download images. Put text links as captions next to or underneath buttons. US email consultancy Silverpop found that the ideal number of links to maximise click rates was 6-10.

Stiff style

An email is no place for using 'purchase' instead of 'buy'. And your language needs to be less formal because people are used to the informality of email as a communications medium. Plain English, in other words. Even if you're selling subscriptions to a software product aimed at radiographers, you can write copy like this:

> Of course you want to be sure RadiographerWare 3.0 will do all I promise. That's only natural. So here's what I suggest. Try it, free, for a month. Then decide.

Overlong paragraphs

That means virtually all of them. Most people, me included, are used to drafting sales copy in a word processor with page margins set for A4 (US letter). Which is fine if you're printing it out as a sales letter. But for emails, where you should in any case be constraining line length to 12-16 words, what looks like a fairly short paragraph in Word becomes a thick, lardy slab. Where you do break them? Wherever it feels OK to do so. But do it as soon as you can.

Like this.

One-line, one sentence, even, is fine for a paragraph. Remember, your prime aim with paragraphing in copywriting is to train your reader to keep on reading.

Impersonal tone of voice

In direct mail letters, some copywriters feel it's OK to talk about 'subscribers', 'our customers' or 'executives'. (They're wrong.) But in an email, which someone might be reading on their Blackberry or mobile phone, you *must* use a personal style to hook them. Simplest trick I know? Call them 'you'.

Poor subject line

It all happens with the subject line, which we tend to read vertically down our inbox, not horizontally along the line. So place your keywords toward the beginning, preferably in the first two words. The recipient's first name is good, if you have it. This works for e-zines too. Long headlines in print DM work fine, if they're good ones. But for email, you want them as short as possible. Shorten individual words – 'business' becomes 'biz'; strip out padding words like 'the' and 'that'.

Long sentences

This is a problem for all sorts of copy, not just digital. But for emails, forcing your reader to plough through long sentences will result in them giving up. It's just too hard. So aim for around ten words per sentence on average. Fewer if you can make it work. But always bear in mind the reader and their expectations. I wrote an email for a business intelligence company with an average sentence length of 10.4.

What you must include

You have to include everything you need to get your reader to take the desired action. If you're emailing pro skateboarders with a download of a new skateboard game and the chance to win a free trip to the Xtreme Games, maybe 20 words will do it.

Dude! It's here. And it's awesome.
Reece Dunwoody's ProSkate 5.
Check it out. Download the first level now free.
Reece

If, on the other hand, you're contacting finance directors about a new approach to corporation tax that will require them to attend a seminar and ultimately spend £50,000, you may find you need to include a little more information.

In this, nothing has really changed from the old-school direct mail letter-writing guidelines. Say everything you have to say, then stop. But if anything, you have to be even more rigorous at the editing stage in pruning every last word that gets in the way of a clean transmission of your sales message. I recently went through a 277-word email and took out almost 10%. No major words, just filler.

In talking to various people to prepare this section, many recommended including more than one call to action, sprinkled through the text. This is sound advice I'm happy to repeat. If your reader is only skimming and scanning, then restricting yourself to a single hyperlink or button is unnecessarily tight. Put them wherever the reader is going to look, in the hope that at least one will catch their eye.

In terms of content, the rule is the same for sales letters. Lots of benefits; answers to any objections (there may be none, as in the skateboard example above); some form of reassurance like a testimonial or endorsement; and just enough detail about your product to get them to do whatever you want them to.

What you can leave out

Much of what I say in the chapter on sales letters applies here too. It's common sense that you don't need to tell people stuff that is irrelevant to the subject or required action. If we call this section What you *must* leave out, then we're into the area that probably causes emailers more sleepless nights than anything else: spam.

You can download lists of words or phrases that trigger spam filters. I Googled this one in seconds: http://www.wilsonweb.com/wmt8/spamfilter_phrases.htm. But a careful reading of the accompanying text reveals that these are words you should *consider carefully* before using, not avoid altogether.

The current version of the widely used SpamAssassin software, which is incorporated into lots of different email checking programs, has 746 separate tests for spam. These rules include:

Subject says 'replica'
Body talks about meds and %
Body includes phrase: lower your monthly payments

You can see them all for yourself at
http://spamassassin.apache.org/tests_3_2_x.html.

Interestingly, none specifically forbids the use of the word 'free'. Yes, combined with certain other words it can trigger a spam point, but it's not as clear cut as some would have you believe. The best advice is to behave like an ethical mailer, which you are, I hope, then test your email using any of the freely or commercially available spam check applications.

Leaving spam to one side, you have to focus like a laser on getting your point across in as few words as possible. The key phrase there is 'as possible'. You may need no more than 20 words. You may need 100. Or 2,000. Just make sure each one is vital, and that to leave it out would diminish the power of your email.

How to structure it

First a quote from a client on the subject of long copy:

'You personally brain-washed me into long copy, and I have never found shorter copy perform better, even in email!'

Note that she says 'perform better' – there's no reference to what she 'likes'.

Second, is your email designed to look like a personal communication, or more of an online flyer?

If it's the first, you'll want to go for a single-column HTML template or the plainest of HTML designs to replicate the look and feel of plain text. I've seen both used very effectively. If it's the second, you have more scope, design-wise, but I think these are less successful, mostly because they are instantly recognizable as both promotional in content and impersonal in style. Neither very strong reasons to open or read. Yet people keep using them, so they've found something that works for them.

From field

If you have a well known brand name, either use that in the From field, or stick it after a comma and your name. Like this:

From
Andy Maslen, Sunfish

Subject line

We've more or less covered this already, but to reiterate the 'rules' for good subject lines:

1. Make sure you use keywords that your reader would use themselves if they were, for example, searching the web for articles on the same subject. This search engine optimisation (SEO) route is a good one because it makes you see the world from your reader's perspective.

2. Use those keywords at the very start of your subject line. Research shows that email clients like Outlook and Gmail truncate subject lines at 35 to 40 characters. So leaving your keywords to the end, or inserting them in the middle could be fatal to your open rate.

3. Keep your subject line short, say under 40 characters. Or don't, because as in every field of human endeavour, there are two sides to this debate. Some testing has revealed higher open rates for subject lines in the 70-80 character range, although this might be working better for e-zines, where there's a stronger relationship between sender and recipient.

4. Make sure that you are signalling something of benefit to the reader. This one makes me laugh. Why? Because although I'm sure the directors of the new breed of e-marketing best practice consultancies have read their advertising history books, it's always presented as brand new wisdom. 'After extensive testing, we concluded that the subject lines that yielded the highest open and click-through rates promised the reader some kind of benefit at the start.' Er, OK, this is what's known in the trade as the science of the bleedin' obvious. I think we already knew that benefits worked for ad headlines and sales letters so why the breathless announcement? It is true. But it was *always* true.

5. Test using your recipient's name. You could collect first name or first name and surname, and you could test using both.

Headline

Your recipient may be looking at your email in the preview pane, using it as a quick tool to decide whether to read the whole message, ie open it. If your prospect has their reading pane switched on, they'll see the top of your message without opening the email. So use a headline, make your offer prominent, have a call to action or all three.

What do we know about headlines that work in emails? Pretty much the same as we know about headlines anywhere else. They should appeal directly to the reader's self-interest ie they should promise a benefit of some kind. They should be personal, urgent, practical, irresistible, specific and, please, related to the promise, not the picture (if you have one).

You can use your headline as a hyperlink to a landing page too. Why wait till the end of the message before asking for the order? They may just do it straight away.

Salutation

It's an old-fashioned word for a chapter on writing email copy. It just means

Dear Andy

Or

Dear Mr Maslen

Leave it out and you fail the first test of personal writing. If you haven't collected the data – though that leads to the question, is your list opted-in? – you could say:

Dear Classic Car Owner

Or

Dear Saver,

(Dear Friend, the spammer's favourite, is best avoided.)

First paragraph

One thing to consider when you're writing your opening sentence, which may be your entire opening paragraph...

Do. Not. Waffle.

Get straight to the point. Even if it feels more abrupt than you would be in a sales letter. The context is different and you need to reflect that in the way you write. If you have a new piece of software for chartered accountants that will save them and their practice thousands of pounds a year, that's what you should start with.

Second and subsequent paragraphs

Now build on your opening paragraph. Explain, briefly, why they should do what you're asking them to. You can explain the benefits in more detail. You can provide credentials. You can offer a testimonial or two. But be succinct. Edit ruthlessly.

And if your copy is longer than a half-dozen lines, consider using multiple calls to action. You can vary the way you write them, but make sure each one is a hyperlink if you're looking to close the sale online. If you want them to email you or call you, the same basic rule applies.

Sign-off

Here's how you sign off an email:

Kind regards,

Andy Maslen
Managing Director

Not:

Kind regards,

Sunfish

Or, worse:

Kind regards,

The Sunfish Team

Legal stuff

Right at the bottom, you have all the small print where you tell them why they are receiving this email and what to do if they want to stop receiving emails from you.

Notes on style and tone of voice

Keep it personal, keep it friendly, and keep it as informal as you dare. You might be writing to senior executives or justices of the peace, but you can still afford to use a lower register than you might in a business letter. It's just the way email is.

Long strings of adjectives might work in print (I'm not sure they do) but they tend to deaden any power your copy has in digital media. It slows comprehension down and flattens your tone. Sounds very boastful and unengaging too. So instead of writing, 'Our research is insightful, comprehensive, detailed and up-to-date and will help you make better IT purchasing decisions, faster,' you could just say, 'Our research helps you buy the right IT for your business. Faster'.

In the past I have railed against 'click here', arguing that the presence of hypertext itself signals click here. But the digital world never stands still and I have some evidence now that asking your reader to click on the link improves click-through rates. It's worth testing.

Back in the day, we were told we had five seconds to grab our prospect's attention with a sales letter. Now, with emails, it's probably a tenth of that. Waffling was always a high-risk strategy; it's unsustainable now. You can get into detail, but you have to work the detail harder. Chop it up and use short, tight language. If there's so much to say you feel uncomfortable including it all in an email, go to a landing page to finish the pitch.

> Keep it personal, keep it friendly, and keep it as informal as you dare.

Using images

Be mindful that not all the people on your list will be able to see images in emails. So make sure they're not essential to understanding your copy. Make sure, also, that they are *relevant*. Images that show the product are good. If it's a personal email, your own ugly mug might be just the job. Stay away from the panoply of library images that everyone's seen a million times before. Just now, emailers seem to be fond of brightly coloured fruit for some reason – I'm seeing a lot of limes and lemons. Funky-looking people pulling faces are another stock-in-trade. But all they do is say, 'no original thinking here'. Avoid.

Figure 10 HTML blast email for *The Grocer* magazine.

Compare this to the sales letter from the same campaign in Chapter 2. Much of the same copy and branding but repurposed for the online medium.

Online, sans serif typefaces are easier to read – the opposite of print.

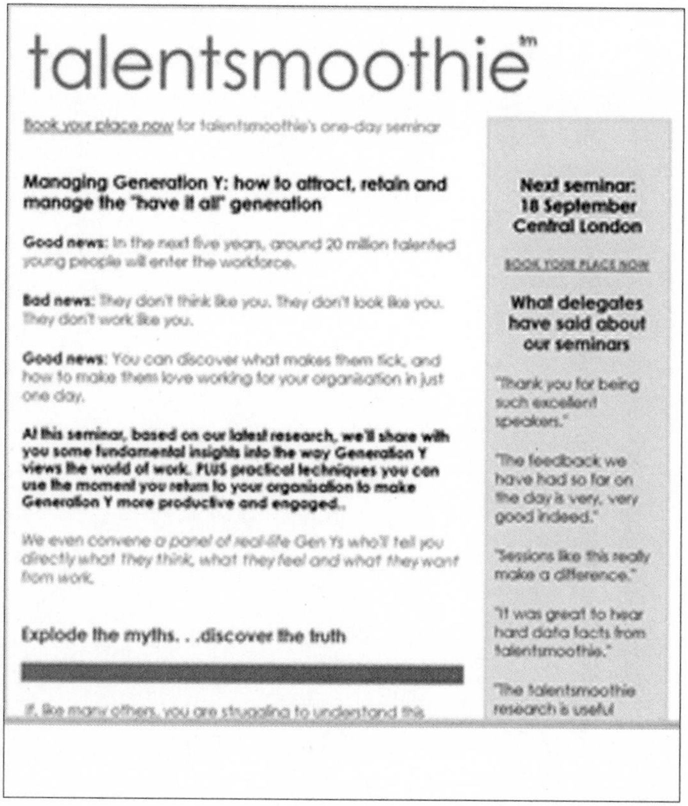

Figure 11 HTML blast email for consultancy talentsmoothie

A different approach but still lots of reasons to buy and an early call to action.

CHAPTER 11
ADWORD

MAGNETIC ADWORDS
COPY? TOP WEB
COPYWRITER
SHOWS YOU HOW
TO MAX OUT
YOUR ADWORD
CONVERSIONS
WWW.SUNFISH.CO.UK

Introduction

If you're not sure, AdWords are those four-line text items you get down the right-hand side of the page when Google gives you your search results (and above the search results). You'll hear people talking about 'natural' search and 'paid' search. The former refers to the results you get when Google searches for websites containing text (keywords) that matches your search term: gym ball, HR consultants or Cornish surf holidays. The latter are the hits returned when Google searches all the AdWords that the owners of those websites have written and paid for.

AdWords are like any other form of copywriting: they're there to grab your attention and persuade you to take an action. The difference between AdWords and traditional advertising is twofold:

a) the action is always the same, for every advertiser: click on the ad
b) you only pay if the reader of your ad takes the desired action

As with direct response advertising, AdWords would have made Lord Leverhulme, who, famously, didn't know which half of his advertising budget he was wasting, much happier. For one thing, the only money he would have been spending *at all* would have been for actions caused by his ads. And for another, he could have then gone on to track those ads that led to sales, ie the conversion rate. And it's this ratio – the proportion of clickers who turn into buyers – that is the ultimate test of an AdWord's effectiveness. Because, just as the point of a press ad isn't to get as many people as possible to read it, the point of an AdWord isn't to have as many people as possible click it. It might feel like it is, at least, at the beginning. But once you start counting the cost of the clicks that don't convert – the so-called abandonment rate – the penny drops (out of your pocket and into Google's).

As with the section on emails, I am going to limit myself principally to a discussion of AdWord copywriting. An entire industry has grown up around the art and science of AdWords,

If you're not sure, AdWords are those four-line text items you get down the right-hand side of the page when Google gives you your search results.

from how much to bid for keywords to the right way to schedule them. If you want to get into that and buy the DVDs, you may get an edge. But, as with all advertising, you gotta have the copy first.

Strengths

AdWords are great because they allow you to compete on fairly level terms with everybody else and because you only pay for what you get – at least as far as delivering visitors to your site. It's a mistake to think of them as cheap though. If you write a brilliant ad in terms of attracting eyeballs, you may be getting hundreds or thousands of clickthroughs every day of the week. But if you're not converting them, you're paying a fortune…. for nothing.

On some AdWords campaigns I ran to drive subscriptions to my e-zine, the click-through rates (CTR) ranged from 0.02% to 1.41%. The conversion rate ranged from 2.38% to 25%. A few moments on Google itself searching for 'typical AdWords conversion rates' yielded stats of anywhere between 3% and 5% as an average conversion rate.

You have to decide what constitutes a reasonable amount to pay for each sale – in that respect it's no different from any other marketing expenditure. You set your budget, measure your sales and calculate the return on investment (ROI). As long as you're happy, you keep going, refining your ad to try to up the conversion rate.

The real strength of AdWords isn't their cost – it's their measurability. You can test – and measure – everything, from time of day the ads are served (shown) to the price you bid for the keywords linked to your ads. And, of course, endless variations of headline, copy and landing page.

Weaknesses

Shall we start with the obvious? AdWords are really, *really* short. We'll come on to just how short in the section on structuring your copy. That means you have to be very precise in your copy and objectives. Is that really a weakness? Maybe it's a strength. The more complex your proposition, the more you're going to struggle to sell it through AdWords. Though given what you're trying to do is drive people to your website/landing page, where the real selling gets done, it should be possible to write an ad that will do that whether you're selling paperclips or jet engines, office cleaning or management consultancy.

Like any form of advertising, AdWords demand that you track how you're doing. They do it more than, let's say, press advertising (the non-direct variety, that is), because it's quite possible to run unprofitable press ads for years. (It's not sensible, but it is possible.) But the nature of AdWords advertising means you *are* going to be worrying away at your CTR and conversion rates because they make it so simple. And every time you pay that bill at the end of the month, you're going to see *exactly* how much money you've spent for *exactly* what return. Kind of focuses your mind. Sorry, that's also not really a weakness.

OK, one last go. The real weakness of AdWords is that they are not a one-stage sell unlike, say, direct response advertising. They can't be. There's no call to action, no order form, no number to call. The reader has to make a second step. And the abandonment rate can be pretty steep, as the figures above show. Driving people (traffic) to your website is *not* the goal of AdWords any more than driving awareness is of press advertising.

What can you use it for

A shorter section would be called 'What can't you use it for?'. You can use AdWords for pretty much anything. Selling products, generating sales leads, registering visitors to your website, offering downloads: they can all work. I spent a few, weird, minutes Googling the following random searches and found they all had AdWords attached:

1. Architects
2. Beach houses
3. Compost
4. Diving equipment
5. Electroplating chemicals
6. Food additives
7. Greenhouse gases
8. High-output turbocharger
9. Ink cartridges
10. Juicer
11. Knight costume
12. Lugnuts
13. Massage therapy
14. New age music
15. Optometrists
16. Plastic surgery
17. Quiz ideas
18. Rolling road
19. Strategy consultant
20. Tree surgeon
21. Underwear
22. Victorian antiques
23. Water birth
24. X-ray machine
25. Youth theatre
26. Zoo keeper

The key is to have a very definite action you want from your visitor *once they get to your site*. Don't just send them to your home page. Have what's called a landing page – a specific page created just for your AdWord campaign where the action requested or flagged up in the ad is taken by the visitor. If you promise a free report on home hair colouring, send them to a page where that's what they get *if* they give you their name and email address, not a general page about all your home salon treatments and products.

What goes wrong

There are only two things that really go wrong with AdWord campaigns. Problem one: you don't get any clicks at all. So although it hasn't cost you any cash, (though it might have cost you plenty of time), you're not making any money either. Problem two: you're getting loads of clicks and no, or too few, conversions. Now it has cost you plenty of cash and you're *still* not making enough money.

With the first problem, assuming you have chosen the right keywords and bid the right amount of money – Google is very good at helping you with this, perhaps not entirely selflessly – the problem comes down to the wording of your AdWord. It's simply not grabbing attention, despite its position on the page, or else it is grabbing attention but the next couple of lines fail to excite the reader into taking any further action.

With the second problem, you can clearly write an enticing ad but you're losing all your customers before they buy/register or do whatever it is you want them to. So the problem is down to your landing page. Is there a mismatch between what your ad promises and what the landing page delivers? The thread binding your visitor to you is gossamer thin, so even a superficial difference between ad and landing page, like promising a free report then offering a free monthly e-zine, could be enough to put them off. Maybe your form or shopping basket looks dodgy or incomplete in some way. Perhaps you need to have a more prominent privacy policy. Maybe your prices are too high.

In terms of copy, Google imposes very tight rules on what you can and can't say, and especially on how long you have to say it. It's not secret or mysterious, in fact you can't even save your ad until it complies with Google's rules. But it does mean you have to master this ultra-tight copywriting style. If you only have 25 characters for a headline, words like 'the' and 'that' begin to look like real luxuries. We'll come onto style and structure in a moment.

What you must include

Google works on the principle of relevance. If people are searching for organic seed compost, Google wants to return websites and AdWords that deal specifically with organic seed compost. Not organic seeds or seed compost or compost generally, but 'organic seed compost'. That means you need to not only bid for the most specific and relevant keywords you can think of (and once again, Google will help you), you also have to include them in your copy.

You also need to figure out, then meet, your target reader's expectations. Imagine them sitting at their desk, or on their sofa, searching the Internet for the thing you can provide. What need are they trying to meet? What problem are they trying to solve? What itch are they trying to scratch? And then, this question...

What are they going to type in?

Someone suffering from painful joints in their fingers might type in 'joint pain' or 'hand joint pain' or 'pain relief hands'. They might put 'carpal tunnel syndrome' because they think that's what they've got, even if they haven't. You might be selling heated gloves that do, genuinely, provide pain relief for arthritic finger joints. But it's unlikely your reader is going to be typing 'heated gloves' because they don't know they exist. So, don't think of the solution (your view of the world), think of the problem (your reader's view of the world).

Lesson two, get the facts in. Make it crystal clear what you're

> Don't think of the solution (your view of the world), think of the problem (your reader's view of the world).

selling. It's back to those keywords again. If you're selling scuba equipment, talk about that. If you're selling face masks and snorkels, that's even better. There's so little space, you are freed from trying to create word pictures or any of the other more involved copywriting techniques you can employ in longer copy forms like sales letters and press ads. All you have space for is the product, the need it meets and maybe an offer of some kind.

And try to offer a benefit too. This is really copywriting 101. You have to think in terms of the benefits of what you're offering. Someone who's short of cash and is looking for a way to cut their debts is more likely to respond to an ad promising 'freedom from debt' or 'no more money worries' than one talking about 'debt consolidation' or 'debt refinancing'. This is old ground and I don't propose to go over it again here in detail, but you must include some appeal to your reader's self-interest. Because space is at such a premium in an AdWord, that appeal and the language you couch it in is going to be pretty basic.

What you can leave out

Given the severe restrictions on space, you have to follow William Strunk Jr.'s dictum and 'omit needless words'. Generally speaking, needless words can be identified because when you take them out your message remains unchanged. (Actually, your message is stronger without them.) In AdWords copywriting, it's all the little joining words that help 'normal' copy flow, but which you simply can't afford here.

Imagine you were trying to stop someone getting on a train just by yelling something at them. You're competing with tannoy announcements, whistles and the general hubbub of a railway station. That's the level you need to be thinking at for AdWords copy.

In the old days, people would send telegrams to each other when they couldn't wait for the normal post. You paid for every single word so the style became terse. That's good practice for AdWords.

Here are a few specifics of what to leave out:

Long words – sounds obvious, but when your longest line is only 35 characters including spaces, words like 'significant' are pointless when 'big' or 'huge' are available.

Jargon – what's obvious to you might be nonsense to your reader. Avoid 'ROI' in favour of 'profit' even if the meaning isn't 100% the same, *unless* you're certain everyone you want to click knows the jargon in question.

Excessive punctuation – Google isn't mad keen on spammy-looking ads so those triple exclamation marks are out, I'm afraid.

Superlatives – don't bother calling your product 'exciting', 'fantastic' or 'unique'. If it *is* any of those things, the name or description will prove it. If it isn't, you won't convince your reader just by sticking the words in your ad.

How to structure it

There's only one way to structure your AdWord and that's the way Google tells you to. That makes my job fairly simple. Here's a screenshot from Google that shows you what they want.

Let's try an exercise. Suppose you are selling your services as a sports injury therapist and personal trainer. Here are a few headlines that might work in print (don't forget the spaces count as characters too):

Andy Maslen offers sports injury therapy, massage and personal training
Get yourself into shape this Spring
Strains, sprains and pains: let me treat you
Beer belly? Get rid of it with your own personal training programme
Win the Dads' race this year

They all might work in print, but none of them will in an AdWord. They're all too long.

Here are a few that might work…

Sports injury therapy [21 characters]
Personal trainer [16 characters]
Sports massage [14 characters]
Your sports injury cured [24 characters]
Sports therapy training [23 characters]

Not exactly what you'd call creative are they? But they are exactly the sort of lines or keywords that your target customer is typing into Google.

Your next two lines are where you expand on your promise. But there's so little space that you have to stick to your core message. If you offer a local service, you can qualify that with the town or city name where you operate. Or you can go into more detail about the product or service you provide. So, returning to our sports injury therapist, you could write:

Sports injury therapy
Andy Maslen: massage, ultrasound
Qualified sports therapist W London
www.andymaslen.com

If you're using AdWords to build a list, perhaps for your e-zine, then you have a two-stage sell, where stage one is getting people to sign up, before you pitch products and services to them in the e-zine itself. This is a great technique when you want to keep your brand in front of your target customers without making cold calls or paying repeatedly to advertise to them. I do it for Sunfish, my copywriting agency, and so do thousands if not millions of consultants and experts in everything from Reiki healing to property investment.

What you do here is forget about all the terrific benefits of your service and just focus on the e-zine, white paper or free teleclass you're promoting. Like this:

Free investment tips
Top investor shares techniques
that made me $10 million in 1 year
www.andymaslen.com

The style you need is ultra-short, ultra-concise, ultra-specific.

Notes on style and tone of voice

I think you're pretty much there with style and tone of voice. The style you need is ultra-short, ultra-concise, ultra-specific. I think it helps with tone of voice if you can inject even a little bit of a personal note: anything to lift your ad out of the herd.

You can tell mini stories, as in our ad above. Or you can go for a more factual approach, as for our sports injury therapist. Best of all, you can create ad variations, as Google calls them, where you create and test dozens of different ads all on the same subject and all pointing to the same landing page, then just run them against each other and see which does best.

Google will let you use & instead of 'and'. You can also get creative with regular punctuation to replace whole words or phrases. Here are a few substitutions you could make:

words	punctuation
offers a service including	:
which means that	>
and (in a list)	,
plus	+
when you	-
I can help you to	capital letter on next word

Using images

You can't.

CHAPTER 12
ARTICLE

COPYWRITER
ANDY MASLEN
GIVES HIS TIPS
FOR SUCCESSFUL
ARTICLE WRITING

Introduction

If you get asked to write an article, well done! It's one of the best ways to promote yourself and your business. Readers respect and trust what they read in magazines, websites and newspapers far more than adverts, mailshots and websites (the corporate ones, anyway). Maybe you suggested (pitched) an article idea to a magazine editor and they said yes. Perhaps, because of your reputation in your field, an editor approached you. Or did your PR agency swing it? It doesn't matter really, as long as you can deliver. But for many marketeers, copywriters and entrepreneurs, the more journalistic style required for articles is unfamiliar ground.

Happily for you, though, the research is fairly undemanding (the research into the appropriate style, I mean). All you need to do is settle down with a few back issues of the journal in question and … read them. In fact, research is the key to a good article. The ideal situation is to have a surfeit of facts, so that you are free to pick and choose what you include.

As you're reading this chapter in a book about copywriting, rather than journalism, I'm going to assume your main interest in articles is for their value as a PR tool. That means you're unlikely to be worrying too much about whether you get paid to write it. Which is just as well, because, generally, editors feel that the free PR you get is ample reward for your efforts. You may get a fee, but it won't be much, maybe a couple of hundred pounds or a free ad in exchange. I would always grab any article offer with both hands and see it as a delayed return on investment.

Strengths

The huge strength of an article is its perceived neutrality, or independence. You benefit from the implied endorsement of the magazine, or website or newspaper. In return, you have to *be* neutral. More of that in a moment. Within the PR industry, the standard valuation of editorial is three times the cost of the equivalent amount of advertising. It's called 'advertising equivalent value'. So if you're asked to write a one-page article (the brief will specify a word-count but let's assume it'll fit on one page), it's worth 3x, where x is the rate-card price for a full-page ad in the same magazine.

It's also an opportunity to change down a gear from the sales copy you're more used to writing. You can relax a bit and write to interest people, rather than purely to persuade them. Obviously, your ultimate aim is to do just that, but this is more about brand promotion or reputation management than hardcore selling.

You can also multiply the value of your article by requesting reprints and including them in sales kits, placing a framed copy in your reception area (if you have a reception) and by reproducing excerpts in your corporate brochure. And remember to let your clients know you've done it and where they can read your piece.

Weaknesses

In return for the glow of independent endorsement of your views, you have to surrender virtually all control over the timing and ultimate shape of your article. It may well come out when the editor said it would, in pretty much the same form as you wrote it. But it might not. Editors have no compunction about holding a story over until another issue if something more interesting/relevant/newsworthy comes along. If space is short in that particular issue, or they feel you're going on too long, they'll cut it, sometimes drastically. You can't be too precious about your article. It happens to real journalists all the time and you just learn to live with it. If it gets really hacked about, the editor probably didn't like it. Be grateful it got used at all and swallow your pride.

The style and approach editors require means your article will not work well as an ad for your business. Or not directly anyway. You will emerge as a credible industry voice and you will usually get some sort of signpost at the end of the article pointing to your website, your email address or your phone number, maybe even a one-line profile of your organisation. If you want to blow your own trumpet, it's simple: buy an ad, or that bastard child of advertising and journalism, the advertorial. For me, though, there's something a little dispiriting about those wannabe articles with the fateful word ADVERTORIAL or ADVERTISEMENT looming over the headline. They might as well put a sign up saying, 'skip this, it's an ad in disguise'. On the other hand, as discussed elsewhere in this book, I love the idea of an ad that follows editorial conventions. And sometimes, if you haven't explicitly booked an advertorial, the ad department are happy to run it without the ADVERTISEMENT tag. But back to articles...

> The main use of an article is to enhance your reputation and gain positive PR for your business.

What can you use it for?

The main use of an article is to enhance your reputation and gain positive PR for your business. It's a platform you can use to expound your opinions, expertise or experience to the people you hope will buy from you. Who are your audience? Existing customers, who will feel gratified they're doing business with someone important enough to write articles in 'their' magazine or newspaper. Potential customers, who now have an independent endorsement of your business. Even ex-customers, who may feel they misjudged you and could try you again. Not to mention, employees, suppliers, your bank, your auditors and all the other stakeholders in your business who will notch up their opinion of you.

In practical terms, you can say that readers will be more likely to do the following after reading your article:

• Enquire about your products or services.
• Visit your website or landing page.
• Try your service or product.
• Add you to a pitch list.
• Invite you to tender for a project.
• Hire you to do some work for them.

Broadly speaking, though it's not particularly easy to measure, people are more likely to view you favourably and, by extension, your other more directly commercial communications such as emails, mailshots and advertising.

What goes wrong

Not relevant to reader

Whether or not you're being paid to write the article, your prime duty is not to your PR agency, your shareholders or even the editor of the publication or site you're writing for. It's to your reader. This goes for all the copywriting tasks in this book (with the possible exception of e-zines) but it goes double for articles. Why? Because this is the only communications channel where your reader has *chosen* to read your copy in the expectation of learning something, or being entertained. People do *kind* of choose to read emails or sales letters, but their mindset is completely different. They know they're being sold to and in many cases are reading virtually against their will.

The simple solution is to read a few back issues of the publication you're writing for. If it's a website, read other posted articles. This will help you write in the right style if you've been commissioned to write an article, and to pitch your ideas to the right media outlet if you're doing it speculatively. A magazine that already has a copywriter as a monthly columnist is unlikely to want another one. A marketing and advertising magazine is unlikely to take an article on procurement or IT. Unless it's marketing IT.

Corporate puff

'Wow! I've got 1,500 words to pitch my company to potential customers' is a fairly typical reaction of many first-timers on being commissioned to write an article. Er, no. You've got 1,500 words to meet the brief supplied to you by the editor. It will talk about the content of the article and the aims (see 1, above), and it will stipulate that you must not use your article as a platform for corporate horn blowing. Editors are hyper-vigilant about protecting the editorial integrity of their publications – and after all, that's why you want to be in there in the first place. So please resist the temptation to talk about your 'unique customer-facing solutions' and 'best-of-breed product portfolio'. It'll only get cut and you'll damage, perhaps fatally, your relationship with the editor you worked so hard to cultivate.

Too short

The brief will include a word limit: 400, 1,600, 3,000, whatever. Stick to it. If you underwrite they will come back to you asking for the rest of it. Now you have to interpolate new material after you've stopped thinking about it, and you've put the editor to extra trouble. Not good.

Too long

And try not to go over, either. An acceptable amount would be 10% of what's called overmatter. For a 500-word piece you can afford to write 550, for a 2,000-word piece, nobody will get peevish if you supply 2,200. You may feel, having done your research and written it up, that you can't honestly do it justice in less than 2,500 words. In which case, tell the editor when you send in your copy. Explain your reasons, and offer to cut it, if they want you to.

Don't know the house style

Most media have their own house style rules. Find out what they are and stick to them. It could be something as simple as whether they prefer single or double quotes for quotations. Whether they prefer the present tense for features and the past tense for analysis. Their attitude to addressing the reader directly ('you'). Or whether it's acceptable for the writer to use 'I'. The larger titles will have sub-editors, the smaller ones will rely on the editor to tidy it up. But why put them to the bother? Follow their rules and you become one less thing they have to worry about. You might be commissioned to write more, just because your copy needs so little work to make it fit for the page.

Wrong style for the medium

Print journalism generally has a more relaxed style than online. You can use longer sentences, and take a bit more time expanding on your ideas. It's not the style I advocate in this book for sales letters, e-zines and ads and you may be unused to having this degree of liberty. Again, read the publication you're writing for: all the information you need is there in front of you. For articles destined for the web, you can adopt the more direct, punchy style you already use in sales copywriting. The message is different, but the style is the same. Short sentences. Short words. Bullet points. Quick bites of information that are easy to take in.

Wrong timeframe

If you're writing for a daily or weekly title, you need to be topical; there must be a news hook. For a monthly or quarterly title, topical references date too quickly to be of much use. Talking about things that happened 'this week' won't make much sense if the article appears six months after you wrote it.

Badly written

A bit vague and ragbaggy, this one. But bear in mind that the first person who reads your article is a journalist (editor, writer, whatever you want to call them). Words are their stock in trade and they don't take kindly to people who misuse the language. So check your spelling, punctuation and grammar. Or have someone you trust check it for you.

Missed deadlines

Three words if you're writing for a print publication or an e-zine.

Don't. Do. This.

Press days are sacred and if you miss the deadline bad things happen. For a start, the editor now has a hole they have to fill. For a finish, you will royally piss them off and they will find someone else to write the next article they need from a specialist in your field.

You have more leeway if you're writing for a website but it's still good practice, if not elementary good manners, to deliver on time.

What you must include

Usually, the editor will have given you a written brief for the article. That means you know what they're expecting you to include in your article. Or you will have suggested a topic and maybe an outline of an article to an editor and they've accepted it. Either way, you have a fairly clear idea of what to include. Sometimes there will be an overall point they want you to make, that vending machine pizzas are substandard compared to those made in traditional pizzerias, for example. Then it's up to you to find evidence to make the case. If you discover, as you start your research, that the idea doesn't stand up – perhaps the Pizzamatic turns out perfectly wonderful pizzas, go back to your editor ASAP and explain. They'll rather you do this than slave away trying to write an impossible article and may be happy if you suggest an alternative approach, why auto pizzas are making pizzerias look over their shoulders, for example.

Generally, an article should include information from more than one source. In this sense, it differs from a white paper, which can be all about your business, despite the similarity in writing style. So do your research. If you're a designer writing an article about the design of banks, you should interview a handful of banks and a handful of designers. Unless you've specifically been asked for an opinion or comment piece (which is great, because you can finally unleash that rant you've had building up inside you for years), you should stick to facts. Give your opinions, by all means, but provide evidence for your point of view. 'Banks are designed by intellectual pygmies who care more for awards than customers' is less likely to convince, or interest, your reader than 'many bankers will admit privately, if not in public, that the design of their branches is off the pace compared to supermarkets and even post offices'.

Quotes always work well in articles. If you've interviewed someone and told them you're writing an article for XYZ magazine or website then you've the right to quote them. Generally you're talking to contacts or colleagues so they should be happy to be quoted – after all, they're going to see their name in print too. Make sure you follow house style for the way you attribute and use quotes.

Try to include statistics or other hard evidence to back up your assertions. If I were writing an article about the merits of long copy, I would want to provide client quotes, test results or case studies of A/B copy tests to prove my point. You may be asked to provide bullet points or you may just feel they'll help. These, and quotes or case studies often work well in panel or side-bars: you can indicate to the editor that this is how you think they should be used, but don't be surprised if they decide not to follow your advice.

This might sound obvious, but if you've been commissioned to write a comment or opinion piece, remember to include some opinions, the more forthrightly expressed the better. Avoid lame-sounding openings like 'It could be argued that...', 'There are those who believe that...' and 'Whilst opinions vary, a common thread seems to be that...'. Go for the jugular: 'If you want to write five-word web pages, be my guest. Your designers will be ecstatic; you just won't sell anything'. The dream result for the editor is letters or emails violently disagreeing with your views. It means people have read it (always nice) and engaged with it. You'll probably get asked to write more.

> Quotes always work well in articles.

What you can leave out

When you're editing your first draft, look for passages that seem to be doing any of the following:

- Hyping your company or its products or services.
- Showing off your knowledge rather than drawing on it to make a point.

- Going into too much detail on a technical point.
- Going off the point.
- Talking about stuff you care about but your reader doesn't.

And watch for any of the following:

Empty adjectives: editors will cut all your 'exciting's, 'revolutionary's and 'amazing's. Journalists don't sound breathless about the subjects they're covering, and neither should you.

Redundant language: don't bother talking about 'important developments', 'close scrutiny' or 'orange in colour'. They'll just get cut to 'developments', 'scrutiny' and 'orange'.

Management speak and business clichés. Your colleagues may love talking about kicking it to the kerb, doing the heavy lifting or slapping the puck, but editors generally despise this type of thing.

Jargon. Unless the jargon in question is universally understood by the magazine's readership, avoid it in favour of plain English. Marketing and advertising people don't even recognise 'above-the-line' as jargon, so you're free to use it in an article for a marketing magazine or website. ROI is fine for general business and financial titles. But be aware that not everyone reading these titles will have much experience, so always spell out more obscure terms first before abbreviating them. The standard form is to talk about return on investment (ROI) the first time you use the phrase, and ROI thereafter.

How to structure it

There are much more detailed books and articles than this one on how to structure features, which I guess you will be writing most often. There are dozens of formal theories about different ways to write journalistically. In general, though, you should aim to introduce the main point of your article in the first paragraph, if not the first sentence. So, follow the old presentation rule of three: tell them what you're going to tell them; tell them; tell them what you've told them.

A good tip from the pros is that your introductory paragraph should be what you'd say to a mate down the pub. If you can't explain it in simple language, you need to go back and do some more thinking. Once you've introduced your point or theme, you can expand on it, introduce secondary points that reinforce it, provide evidence, give other people's opinions – as quotes – and, finally, round it all up, maybe with a final quote or pertinent point.

The finished article, once it's printed or uploaded, will most likely follow a scheme like this:

Headline to catch the reader's eye (it may have been used as is, or slightly altered, as a cover line and in the table of contents).

E.g. I'm not spam, really!

Then a standfirst. This is the short paragraph of maybe a sentence or two that sits between the headline and the body copy. Its job is to entice the reader still further and to summarise the theme or point of the article.

E.g. Writing powerful email copy needs a more delicate touch in today's web-savvy world, says Andy Maslen. Here he gives seven tips for slipping under your reader's radar.

Next, and critically, your opening paragraph. You can pose the problem you're going to deal with, or cite some recent research, tell a story or jump straight in with whatever you want to talk about. Just make sure you leave your reader wanting more. Most people will quickly skim the opening paragraph of an article before deciding whether to carry on. (A bit like sales letters and emails really.)

Follow the old presentation rule of three: tell them what you're going to tell them; tell them; tell them what you've told them.

177

As you get into the article you can relax, on the assumption that your reader is willing to go with you as long as you keep things relevant to them and their needs or interests. It's a good idea to introduce a different viewpoint quite soon after you start unless you're writing an opinion piece. That could be a quote from someone you've interviewed, some statistics or a survey finding.

Once you've introduced your main point, provided evidence for your point of view, expanded on your theme and maybe introduced a second or even third point, you close. You could use a final quote or statistic or summarise your main point.

Finally, be sure to include a short profile and your contact details. The editor might cut it but they're unlikely to, especially if you haven't been paid.

Notes on style and tone of voice

We've already talked about the need to follow house style. That is the over-riding guide to how you should write. You don't want to submerge your personality totally; after all, you were asked to write the article in the first place because of who you are and what you know. But nor should you ignore the flavour and tone of the magazine or website overall.

In general, when writing articles you have more leeway than you do in more overt sales communications. You can use humour or wit in a freer way than you would in a sales letter (if you would at all) and you might want, or be asked, to be entertaining or even provocative.

A personal, conversational tone will often be entirely appropriate for the title you're writing for, where 'you' and 'I' are fine. Just check with the editor and, once again, review the tone and style used in published articles. Let's be even more specific: in published articles in the same section of the magazine, e-zine or site that yours will appear in. Features tend to be more relaxed than news pieces, which should be essentially free of tone or obvious stylistic devices like alliteration, groups of three ideas or sentence fragments (sentence-alikes without verbs); comment pieces are more outspoken than either.

There are some commonly accepted rules for good English style that you'll find in various places, online and offline. Look at the published style guides – *The Economist*, *The Times* (of London), *The Guardian*, *The New York Times*, *The Wall Street Journal* all have them; read manuals and books on writing generally (like *The Elements of Style*, also known as Strunk & White, and *The Chicago Manual of Style*) and on copywriting specifically. Get to know them and you'll be a better and more confident writer generally, and more popular with editors.

Using images

The editor may ask you to supply ideas for images, or the images themselves. Most small-circulation magazines and e-zines won't have the resources to employ picture researchers and will love you for providing high quality images to accompany your article. A few things to bear in mind:

High-quality for print means at least 300 dpi at, say, 10 cm. For digital publications, 72 dpi is fine, as that's screen resolution.

Make sure any images you supply are either copyright-free or come with the appropriate permissions. If you've taken photographs, you own the copyright in them automatically. But if you're taking pictures of people, make sure you have a signed model-release if they are members of the public, or some other form of written permission. Staff photos are pretty safe and many companies have a PR page on their website where you can freely download 'media-approved' images.

Pictures need to tell a story. Samey library shots of businessmen shaking hands will not impress anyone.

And remember to provide captions for any images you do supply. They're another chance to make a point, and people expect them.

Do you make these 7 mistakes in your copy?

Many publishers say that their titles "include…". They should say "give you". Some use humour when they should be selling. Still others refuse to use copy on outers. They're making mistakes, says Andy Maslen, that could be avoided.

I'm lazy. I like to steal successful copywriting ideas from the masters who have gone before me. More than that though, I like to avoid making basic blunders that ruin my copy. Here are a handful that make me shudder.

Mistake #1: No benefits

Many publishers delude themselves that their titles are, variously, 'essential', 'revolutionary', 'unique' or 'best'. When, more truthfully, they might be 'useful', 'new', 'practical' or, merely, 'available'. Instead of resorting to false claims, boasts and hyperbole they should be talking about benefits. I imagine many don't because they:
a) Don't know, or have never paused to work out, what the benefits of their titles really are.
b) Find it too time-consuming (or boring) to imagine the world from their subscribers' point of view.
c) Don't know what a benefit is AT ALL – and so wouldn't be able to explain it in writing.
d) Actually believe customers are going to spend their hard-earned cash on something just because it's described as revolutionary.

Here's what I suggest. First, spend some time looking at your title as your customer would. And asking the kind of questions your customer would ask. The simplest and most powerful of these is, "What's in it for me?" Second, start describing how your reader's life will be more interesting, fulfilling or fun if they subscribe. Third, figure out what your title does that's good and write copy that dramatises this.

you. Then you have to figure out the answers to all their "Yes, but…" questions. Here are three of the most common objections and what to do about them…

● Objection 1 – "It's too expensive"
To be honest, price is rarely the real reason why people won't buy from you. It's a smoke screen for deeper-seated objections. Here's what you do. You demonstrate the value of your title to your reader. Show them how much money they'll save, or make, versus the cost. Talk about their purchase as "an investment". That makes it sound more prestigious and introduces the idea of payback.

● Objection 2 – "I need to talk to someone else"
Here's another classic delaying tactic. So you have to show them what they could lose by hanging back. Time is money, right? And give them testimonials from people just like them – an excellent way to provide that missing conversation and reassurance. Old school sales guys would imply that, surely, their prospect was the one to make the decision. "Oh, I didn't realise your wife made all the important decisions."

● Objection 3 – "I'm not sure I really need this"
If this is what you're hearing, boy have you got some work to do. It means you haven't sold your title to your reader. You haven't convinced them that they will be better off with it than without it. Did you cover every single benefit your title offers? Did you explain with facts just how your reader will benefit? Did you tell a story about life as a subscriber that makes it irresistible? No? OK – well that's your next challenge. You need to take a long hard look at your copy and most importantly at your publication. Identify what it does for your reader and this objection will melt away.

Mistake #3: Careless repetition
This is a common mistake that you commonly see when the writer is dreaming of walking on the common instead of focusing on their copy.

I reviewed, for a publisher, a two-page sales letter that managed to use the word fantastic six times. An offer, however fantastic (and believe me, this really wasn't), begins to seem a little desperate when it is described this way half a dozen times.

The two most common causes are laziness and other people changing bits of your copy without reading what's gone before.

The cure is to read your copy aloud – it pulls you up short on all those repeated words. Plus, be creative. How many ways can you express the concept of half price? Save 50%. Buy one, get one free. You pay for the first one, we'll pay for the next. Just £50 (normal price £100). Save £50.

Mistake #4: Clunky phrasing
I once wrote a subscriptions promotion for a publisher with a phrase introducing a key benefit like this: "As a subscriber to X, you enjoy…" Present tense. Assumptive close. Short and to the point. The editor changed it to, "If you subscribe to X, you will be certain to be

---

Figure 12 Article by the author, published in *InPublishing* magazine.

Compare the structure of this article to the case study in Chapter 3.

Headline, standfirst, cross-heads, illustration, body copy.

This is a magazine that gives its readers lots of useful advice, so I made sure there was plenty of it in this article on subscriptions renewals copywriting.

Because it's very much written from an expert's perspective, I inject as much opinion (supported of course) as I can manage. It's not a textbook!

CHAPTER 13
WEB PAGE

WELCOME TO
OUR WEBSITE
(DON'T EVER
WRITE THIS)

Introduction

The three main types of web page you're likely to be writing copy for are e-commerce/shopping sites, landing pages and full corporate sites. In this chapter I'm going to concentrate on the third of these. I don't just mean 'brochureware' as it's disparagingly called, where the site is essentially static. Your site could be a corporate site but with a call to action at the heart of it – whether that's to try your service, order products, request a demo or free trial, or register for your e-zine. Or a hybrid, where there's a mixture of company information, user areas and buying pages.

So why not focus on the other two?

Writing copy for e-commerce pages is, essentially, catalogue copywriting. You need to be able to write concisely about your products, pulling out the key features and benefits in as few words as possible. And at every stage in the buying process, from adding items to the shopping basket to completing the online form, to confirming payment details and finally the order itself, you need to keep watch for 'What if?' questions that might be popping into your customer's head. Decide how you're going to answer them and do it succinctly and reassuringly so they don't abandon their purchase.

Writing copy for landing pages is not so very different from sales letter copywriting. You're making a direct and very personal appeal to the visitor who's come to you via an AdWord campaign or other link. Often these pages even look like letters – sometimes very old-school letters, complete with underlining, handwritten notes, highlighting and the rest of the direct mail copywriter's bag of tricks. For advice on this style of copywriting, turn to Chapter 2 on the sales letter.

What are you trying to achieve ... and how?

As with larger print projects, such as corporate brochures, it's important that you are involved as early as possible in the process. A typical – maybe simplified – project team will include the client,

> You need to be able to write concisely about your products, pulling out the key features and benefits in as few words as possible.

the web designer and the copywriter. You may be both the client and the copywriter. In any case, the important thing is to decide from the outset on a few key points:

What are you trying to achieve? Back in the old days – say the mid-nineties – most companies were trying to achieve... a website. The collective sigh of relief as the thing went live were audible from the marketing department to the room where the servers were housed. But it turns out, online marketing is the same as offline marketing. You spend some money and you want something back. You measure return on investment (ROI) and you test alternative approaches until you get an acceptable figure. So, is this purely to tell prospective customers about your organisation? Offer information and advice? Sign up subscribers? Sell merchandise? Build a social network? Everything that comes next depends on this decision. So it's worth spending some time to ensure everyone agrees on the purpose of the site.

What information does the client want to include in the website and how is this information going to be structured? This will determine the site-map and the number of levels of information visitors have to click through to get to the deepest level. It also helps to avoid duplication of pages. I worked on a website where the designers had multiple pages with the same title. The question was, were they separate pages with separate content or just links to the same page?

How are you going to convey your main messages? Paradoxically, it doesn't all have to be copy. In brochures you have photos and diagrams. On the web you can add audio, video, animation, interactive quizzes, user forums and blogs. You'll rarely see a site with no words (and if you did, you wouldn't need this book to help build it), but as a writer writing for the web, you need to be alive to the possibilities offered by the medium. Sometimes your job as a copywriter begins to morph into an information design consultant. You are still concerned with communicating messages and eliciting reactions, but now you're recommending appropriate tactics to achieve that, beyond the written word. When I'm writing web copy, I see my job as to interpret the client's business needs and ensure the site delivers. Designers can make the site look nice and work properly, but it's still the words that will, ultimately, inform, influence, persuade and sell.

Strengths

One of the main strengths of the web as a communications medium is that it's increasingly the place people start looking when they want information. Consumers and business people are super-comfortable using the web to research and evaluate organisations and their products and services. It's my view that, as the web becomes ever more dominant as an information and sales channel, the old distinction between offline and online copywriting will disappear. When there is no print any more nobody will talk about web copywriting: it will just be called 'copywriting'. As it was for most of the Twentieth Century. And then we're back to old-fashioned ideas about building rapport with our reader, establishing their motivations, offering solutions to their problems and so on.

The web offers infinite flexibility: if you can dream it up, someone can program it. Your words can appear however you want them to (though as we'll see, this can also be a problem). You can also change copy as your product range, corporate vision or marketing goals change – in real time if you really want.

And it's relatively cheap to launch a site and leave it where everyone can find it, compared to the cost of ink, paper and postage to push your messages out to hundreds of thousands – or millions – of potential customers. But...

Weaknesses

Perhaps the biggest weakness of websites is that although you and/or your client will endlessly visit it, there's no guarantee anyone else will. Among all the hype of pull- rather than push-marketing, somebody forgot to mention that if you build it, they might not come. Now you have to invest, heavily, in promoting it. That could mean spending on AdWords campaigns and creating a whole visitor attraction strategy involving social networking sites, blogs and e-zines. You will certainly want to push the site address through all the other communications channels you use. And you'll want to ensure your site is optimised for search engines (of which more in a moment).

From all the talk about making websites 'sticky' – in other words, encouraging visitors to read more, visit more pages and return more often – you can see the big disadvantage of websites. They are so easy to leave. You just don't feel so connected to a screen full of pixels as you do to a physical, tangible object you hold in your hands. Fewer of your senses are involved, and that is automatically less engaging.

Nor can visitors see everything at one glance. Yes, you have sitemaps, and for more complex sites they can be really useful. But, in all honesty, how many times have you sat looking at a sitemap and said 'Oh yes, that's much easier to figure out now'? The onus is on your designer – and you as the copywriter – to make the site as clear as possible to navigate. Navigation needs to be intuitive and orientated towards the reader's needs not the company's.

What can you use it for?

What can't you use it for? At the top level, you can – and should – use your website to reinforce and complement all the other communications channels you use, online and offline. You can use a website for just about anything you can dream up as a personal or organisational goal. Off the top of my head, and going as fast

185

as I can, here's a list:

- Promote your business.
- Sell your products and services.
- Get people to apply for a job with you.
- Make investors want to buy your shares.
- Push your political views.
- Attack 'unfair' regulation in your industry.
- Sign up new clients.
- Get people to register to join your service.
- Find out more about your customers.
- Get people to sell their stuff through your site.
- Gain new subscribers to your service.
- Deliver your service itself.
- Show how your products work.
- Give examples of successful projects you've undertaken.
- Act as a forum for users to exchange information.
- Build a network of like-minded professionals.
- Create a marketplace.
- Get journalists to write positive stories about you.
- Create a community of people with similar hobbies, interests or ideas.

Pant pant … time to stop.

What goes wrong

Offline copy cut and pasted onto your website

This is the single biggest sin of web copywriting. Or it is unless your offline copywriting is as a good as the best online copywriting. Which in turn should be as good as the best offline copywriting. Confused? OK, let's start again.

Most critics of offline (print) copywriting write from a web perspective. Their beef is that offline copy is dull, or 'send only' and doesn't engage the reader. That's certainly true for *bad* offline copy. But then there's plenty of web copy that stinks too.

The best offline copy (let's choose subscriptions direct mail as a pretty good example) talks *to* the reader not *at* them. It uses everyday language that people can understand without reaching for a dictionary. And it's personal – it sounds like a conversation happening between two equals.

Insincere/impersonal tone of voice

Phrases like 'We at XYZ Corporation…' are pompous and turn visitors off instantly. You can almost hear the self-satisfied tone of voice and see the thumbs hooked into the waistcoat pockets.

Baggy sentences

Online it's a good idea to stick to the shortest sentences you can manage. I'd say for business-to-consumer (b2c) copywriting, 10-12 words per sentence on average is fine. For business-to-business (b2b) copywriting you might get away with a slightly longer sentence: you're not talking to the general population so you can assume your reader is more literate and better educated. But they're also busy and distracted. So aim for around 16 words per sentence. Shorter would be better.

Too many hyperlinks

Yes it's tempting to hyperlink every word or phrase on a page that could conceivably link to another. That was the original intention behind hypertext and you see it a lot on academic sites and Wikipedia. But within a commercial site you are trying to keep your reader with you as you unfold your story. You don't want them to control the direction of travel. I know this flies in the face of the spirit of the Internet but we're trying to sell here, people!

Over-optimised copy

If you pack your copy so tightly with keywords that there's little room for anything else, you might attract more visitors (but see below for what can go wrong) but when they arrive on your page, they'll be instantly turned off by the weird, compulsive repetition of their search term.

If readers of print marketing materials are flighty birds then they're positively jittery online, ready at a moment's notice to slip away to another site, or to check their emails, or Twitter, or their favourite blog. These mistakes will only hasten their departure.

What you must include

What you must include on a web page depends really on what sort of page it is and what you're trying to achieve. Let's say you have an e-commerce page with product descriptions. You need to include enough information about the features and the benefits to make your visitor want to buy it. That means important little details like the price, the dimensions and how they'll get hold of it. You might want to include testimonials right there, next to the product panel to reassure your prospective buyer it's as good as you say it is. And a tight call to action, as text or a button. An 'add to shopping cart' button is always a good one – it's become a standard for the web.

If you're writing a landing page where you're asking someone to stump up a larger amount of cash, maybe for a training course, webinar or online training programme, you'd better include as much, or more, as you would in a long sales letter. All the benefits, with stories that bring them to life. Copy that addresses and resolves your visitor's objections to going along with your suggestion. Testimonials from satisfied (ecstatic would be better) customers. Pictures of the product with captions that aren't just informative – 'Jack Dobbs, World Professional Snake-charmer 2009' – but persuasive as well – 'Sign up for Charmed! and get weekly tips on snake charming from Jack Dobbs, World Professional Snake-charmer 2009 – all for just 99p a week.' And plenty of calls to action, both within the text and as buttons, banners and any other graphic devices you can think of.

If you're writing a corporate site, then each page must include all the relevant information to make the visitor want to progress through the site and do the thing you want them to. That could be case studies, more testimonials, stories from your current employees, details of how your products work, what makes them special, your history and qualifications to offer the service you do and so on.

Headlines

I've read very earnest white papers from web design agencies where the reader is exhorted to write a headline for every page of their site. And that the headline should engage the reader and offer a benefit of some kind. Way to go, braniac!

It's not that it's bad advice. It's just that it's not very new. Or not to any copywriter who's ever written an ad or a sales letter.

There a lot of debate about web page headlines as to whether they should stand alone or should reflect back to the visitor the link they used to get there. If you click on a button called 'About Us' and arrive at a page headed 'Company Profile' there's a momentary pause while you figure out whether the two phrases are synonymous. As we know, a moment is long enough to click away from the site altogether.

My opinion? If you haven't been too creative with your page heads, it's better to go with a line that adds meaning to the micro-text of a button label. You can have it both ways with a headline like this, for an Our Services link:

Our Services: online copywriting that converts more visitors

Keywords

Search engine optimisation (SEO): how long have you got? This is a subject too huge to cover exhaustively in a chapter within a book like this. There are workbooks, e-books, real books, e-zines, blogs, white papers, discussion forums … all devoted to the end-lessly fascinating and critical subject of SEO.

Essentially, you're trying to create a page that is more relevant to the target visitor than any other page on the web. So when search engines spider your page they give it the number one spot in their natural search results whenever a punter enters a particular search term. At its simplest, you first have to identify the keywords and phrases that people are typing into Google and the rest when they are looking for the products and services that you provide. Then weave them, skilfully, into your copy so that your keyword density (the ratio of keywords to all the others) is high enough to register with the spiders.

An example of how not to do it would be:

> Our boutique hotel in Kingston is one of the finest boutique hotels in Kingston. If you're looking for a boutique hotel in Kingston this Kingston boutique hotel is the boutique hotel in Kingston for you.

A better version would be gentler:

> If you're looking for a boutique hotel in Kingston, try The Manse. It's a boutique hotel with a difference. All the intimacy you'd expect, but with the luxuries of a much larger hotel.

I'd say, optimise for your visitor first and search engines second. In other words consider your visitor's reaction to your copy as being the most important factor. You can always find ways to get more traffic to your site, but if the copy you're using turns them off, or away, you're wasting your money.

What you can leave out

Like every other form of copywriting, web pages suffer from the inclusion of the following:

- Jargon – 'We are replatforming our service offering to better serve your needs'.
- Windy phrasing – 'Our aim at this time is to research and disseminate best practice in our core competencies'.
- Long words where shorter words are available – 'we despatch

[send] your goods the same day'.
- Clichés – 'we work hard and play hard'.
- Hype – 'this exciting new greenhouse'.

In general, if it doesn't sound like your best sales person talking naturally with a customer, leave it out. Even though it's the same person reading your offline brochure as your web page, they are far less tolerant of crappy corporate waffle on the web. It just doesn't feel right when it's jostling for attention with Facebook, Twitter and all the blogs, user forums and other co-operative sites and spaces.

How to structure it

If you're creating a site from scratch and structuring the whole thing, the specific pages you include will depend to a large degree on who you are, what you're trying to achieve and the type of site you're creating. But each main type of site where copy is a mainstay – e-commerce, landing page and corporate – has a fairly similar underlying structure that includes some or all of the following:

e-commerce
Product pages
Checkout and payment pages
Discussion boards
Corporate background
Terms and conditions
Privacy policy

Landing page
(Similar to a print sales letter.)
Headline
Sub-head
Salutation
Opening paragraph where you grab them with your main benefit

If it doesn't sound like your best sales person talking naturally with a customer, leave it out.

191

Proof that what you claim is true
Main body: more benefits and more evidence
Testimonials
The call to action
The PS

Corporate site
Home
About us
Our services/products
Our team
Client area
For investors
Testimonials/case studies
Press
Careers
Corporate social responsibility
Privacy policy
Contact us
Sitemap

Remember that visitors to the site may not be coming in to the home page and then proceeding in an orderly fashion through each successive page on the sitemap. If they're coming via a search engine, who knows which page they'll land on. That means you can't assume prior knowledge on any given page. It doesn't mean you have to repeat the whole company profile on every page, just that you and the designer have to provide enough context, which could simply be a consistent colour palette and the logo in the same place.

Within individual pages of a corporate site, it's worth bearing in mind that although people are much more used to scrolling than they were in the early days of the web, you have to be a very skilful copywriter to keep them reading past the first screen. For this reason, I'd suggest a quick start on every page. Get to the point in as few words as possible then stick a full stop in. Then expand on it. Then maybe use a few bullet points to tell the story in outline and point to further pages via hypertext. Then a couple more short paragraphs to round it off. Think like a journalist. Tell them all the essential information straight away: who, what, where, when and why (and how). That way if they get bored or click away, they take away your most important messages.

If the design has a two or three column grid, you can fit more information onto the page but you also have to work harder because now there are conflicting messages and places to start reading. Make sure the designer delivers nice big signposts to the reader so they can figure out where they're supposed to look first/next.

Notes on style and tone of voice

If you've ever read anything you liked about direct mail or direct response advertising, that's the style to go for. Short concise sentences. Short simple words. Everyday language that people can relate to and that you might hear them using themselves. An emphasis on the reader rather than the writer, which you can achieve by talking to them, using the words 'you' and 'your' more often than 'I' or 'we'.

Try to use the active voice rather than the passive voice. Sentences written in the active voice have the subject then the verb then the object. Or, and far easier to remember: when the actor comes before the action it's the active voice. This gives your website a more vigorous, dynamic feel that simultaneously engages your reader, takes them less time and effort to understand, and uses fewer words.

Aim for a plain English style that uses Anglo Saxon words like 'begin' rather than 'commence', 'cut' rather than 'reduce' and 'pay' rather than 'remuneration'. Avoid fancy language like '*vis-à-vis*', '*de facto*', '*je ne sais quoi*' and '*ad hoc*'. You're impressing nobody and confusing quite a few.

Open each page with a conversational sentence or two that sounds like you talking directly to the visitor. For that reason, I

193

avoid the naff phrase 'Welcome to our website'. You see it every-where but that's no excuse: you see 'as a valued client' everywhere and that's no good either. When you meet a client I bet you say 'Hi', 'Hello', or 'Chris!' not 'Welcome to our offices'. Nor would you start a sales letter with the phrase 'Welcome to our sales letter'. If you really want to welcome people to your website, why not get a picture of a welcome mat and use the line, 'Hey! Great to see you. Come on in'.

The tone you employ is going to depend on the sort of organisation you are and the sort of emotional reaction you want to elicit from your visitor. Going by many misjudged websites, that reaction would be 'Why are you talking like a trendy vicar?' or 'I thought this was a customer-friendly organisation, not the headquarters of the Daleks'. I'd suggest that, at the top level, you aim for a warm, friendly, conversational tone of voice. You know, like you use to real people. You can afford to drop down in regis-ter a couple of ticks because the web is a less formal place than the offline world and people are happy to accept it. That doesn't mean using street slang (or what you might fondly imagine to be street slang) or texting language – just a chattier voice than you'd use in a business letter or printed brochure. Test the tone of voice of your web copy by simply reading it aloud. How does it sound? You'll hear it as faithfully as your visitor will.

Using images

On the web it's really the same as for print communications. Real people are always more engaging than models. Real situations and products are more convincing than library shots. But...

Why stop at images? This is the web we're talking about. Get your multimedia head on and start producing video, audio, animation and the rest. Talk to your designer at the outset of the project to figure out which points will be better made by words and which by other forms of content. Every bit of content will need a caption, call to action or instruction of some kind, so they create more copy. But maybe a two-minute video from a customer will say more than you can in 2,000 words.

The test you use on images for websites is the same as for any other medium: why are we using this image? What purpose does it fulfil? How does using it move our visitor close to you goal? If we take it out altogether, is the page weaker or stronger?

Figure 13 web page from crocus.co.uk a gardening site

This page makes shopping at Crocus look easy and safe – a prime aim for any e-commerce site. The paragraphs are short and broken up by dotted rules, making it even easier to read. And the tone of voice is friendly without being frivolous.

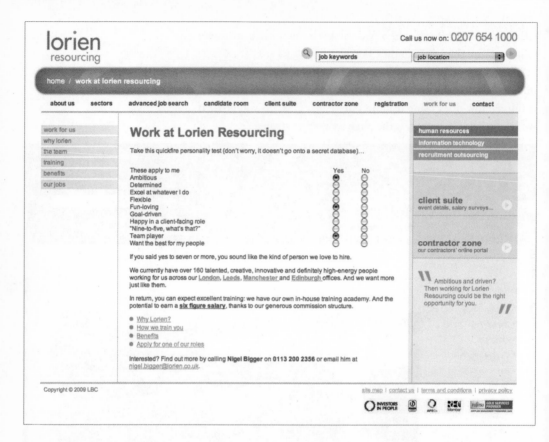

Figure 14 'Work for us' page from Lorien Resourcing, a specialist recruitment company

Web copy doesn't always have to be formal, narrative paragraphs.

This little bit of interactive fun on the Lorien Resourcing site is designed to engage the reader and get potential employees to pre-screen themselves.

CHAPTER 14
ENDPIECE

Well, there you have it. Not everything I could think of – there's nothing in here on writing for TV or radio, or speeches or bid documents. They're either outside my own experience or not strictly marketing or publicity tasks. But if your words appear on paper or screen, I hope you find the guidelines in this book helpful.

There's a lot of crossover too. Postcards are either like very short letters or very long AdWords. Posters are giant headlines. (Unless they're for underground trains or stations where people spend ages looking at them – so you can write a little more.) What works in a sales letter almost certainly works in a sales email or landing page: strip away the delivery channel – the post or the Internet – and you're left with a direct, person-to-person appeal. Articles and white papers share many characteristics, principally their more journalistic writing style, though there are differences. E-zines and old-school newsletters have much in common, as do AdWords and banner/button ads.

I've tried not to repeat myself either. In the sections called 'Using images', I've aimed for constructive advice throughout, rather than just harping on about the clichéd use of library shots – even though this is without a doubt one of the least interesting things you can do with images.

Where I've been able, I've given actual examples of the pieces discussed, from press releases to ads. Another easy way to discover how to write and lay out marketing pieces is to start collecting examples. I have box files in my office groaning with mailshots, case studies, ads and the rest. And remember to keep your eyes open for anything you see over and over again. That means it's working for the company producing it. (Or they are too stupid to notice that their tried and tested mailshot is a dog. Unlikely.)

To close, I thought I'd return to a theme I wrote about in *Write To Sell*, my first book on copywriting: planning. One of my aims in writing this book was to save you time when you're up against a deadline and you have to write something new. The best way I've ever found to save time on a copywriting job is to plan it first. Start with your goals. Then figure out everything you can about your reader. Then decide on the best way to connect their needs to your goals. Don't worry about being 'creative' – save that for your spare time. As David Ogilvy of Ogilvy & Mather once said, 'What you say is more important than how you say it'.

Andy Maslen, Salisbury, 2009.

About the author

Andy Maslen graduated in Psychology and Anthropology from Durham University, in England. He then started work, as a sales representative for a DIY products importer. He also worked as a cook in an Italian restaurant.

In 1986, he began his marketing career, promoting business reports, journals and directories through direct mail. After ten years working in the corporate sector, including a six-year stint as a marketing director, he set up Sunfish, his copywriting agency, in 1996.

Today, he is one of the UK's leading independent copywriters, helping organisations of all sizes build sales and profits through the written word.

Andy is a Fellow of the Institute of Direct Marketing. He writes and speaks regularly on copywriting and co-founded Write for Results, a business writing training company, and Thriving Consultants, a sales and marketing network for self-employed professionals. He also publishes Maslen on Marketing – a free monthly e-zine.

Find out more at www.andymaslen.com.

GLOSSARY

Glossary

abandonment rate – the proportion of website visitors who click a link but then don't follow the order or other desired action through to completion

above-the-line – broadly, brand advertising and other non-measurable forms of promotion such as PR and sponsorship

active voice – a form of sentence construction where the subject precedes the verb, e.g. The writer finished the sentence

ad variation – slightly tweaked version of the same Google AdWord, used to test the effectiveness of different keywords or copy

advertorial – advertisement written and designed to look like editorial, often headed by the word ADVERTISEMENT or ADVERTISEMENT PROMOTION

authoriser – the individual involved in a buying decision who has the power to OK the purchase

banner ad – web advertisement running across the top of a web page or HTML email, wider than it is deep

below-the-line – broadly, measurable marketing activities such as direct mail, direct response advertising and all forms of web-based advertising

body copy – the bulk of the copy in a promotion that sits, usually, below the headline

business-to-business (b2b) – any product or service sold by one company to another, eg management consultancy, office stationery, copywriting

business-to-consumer (b2c) – any product or service sold by a company to consumers, eg cosmetics, lawnmowers, life insurance

button ad – web advertisement on a web page or HTML email, square in format

call-out – a specialised form of caption, often used with product images, where the descriptive or selling text is joined to the image by a thin line, or rule

call to action – any piece of copy that asks the reader to take a specific action, often to place an order

click-through rate (CTR) – the proportion of people who see a hyperlink (in an email, online ad or web page) and click it

conversion rate – any ratio measuring the proportion of leads that convert to sales but on the web specifically, the proportion of people who click a hyperlink and go on to complete the required action, e.g. placing an order or signing up for a newsletter

corporate social responsibility (CSR) – a broad, catch-all term for a range of activities undertaken by companies, that don't lead directly to profit, e.g. environmental, educational, community, diversity or charitable projects

cross-head – a heading that breaks up body copy, in sales pieces or editorial

direct mail – personalised marketing letters, brochures and flyers delivered to consumers and businesses through the post including a mechanism for the recipient to reply directly to the sender e.g. a coupon, web page or number to text

direct response advertising – advertising including a mechanism for the recipient to reply directly to the sender, e.g. a coupon, web page or number to text

embargo – a deadline stated on a press release before which a journalist may not publish its contents

endorsement – praise or recommendation from a respected or well-known figure, though not necessarily one who is a customer

e-zine – a newsletter delivered via email

first person – the style of writing where the writer uses 'I' (first person singular) or 'we' (first person plural)

HTML email – an email incorporating graphics, animation and other design features resembling a web page

hyperlink – any piece of multimedia (text, graphic, etc.) that links to a web page or starts an online action

hypertext – copy in an email or web page, often underlined or in a contrasting colour, that links to another web page or part of one

initial caps – the typographic technique where every word in a sentence or line has the first letter capitalised

keyword – a word likely to be used by people searching for a product, service or company online; used as the basis of pay-per-click advertising such as Google AdWords and in search engine optimisation (SEO)

landing page – a web page linked to a digital promotion such as an email, banner ad or AdWord, or printed marketing materials; often focused on getting the visitor to take a specific action such as signing up for an e-zine

leading – the spacing between lines of type, from the original hot metal typesetting systems when thin strips of lead would be inserted between lines of type to space them out. Tight leading means the lines are scrunched up; loose or relaxed leading means they are further apart

leave-behind – a piece of marketing material, such as a brochure, left with a client by a sales person

library shot – a photograph stored as part of a commercially available collection (usually online) that you can pay to use in a marketing campaign (as can others)

model-release – a form signed by anyone appearing in a photograph that signals their consent for the image to be reproduced commercially

natural search – when web users type keywords or search terms into a search engine and look at the results generated by web pages rather than paid-for web advertising

objection handling – the part of the sales process where the sales person listens to and hopefully resolves the prospect's reservations or doubts about the product or service being sold

opted-in – an email list where each person on it has confirmed that they want to be on it

overmatter – copy that doesn't fit the space allocated to it, either in marketing or editorial environments

paid search – when web users type keywords or search terms into a search engine and look at the results generated by paid-for web advertising rather than web pages

passive voice – a form of sentence construction where the subject follows the verb, e.g. The website was designed by the agency

point size – the distance from the top of the lower case 'h' to the bottom of the lower case 'g' in any given typeface (the standardised conversion is 72 points to the inch)

privacy policy – a statement on a web page that explains what data the site owner holds

pull quote – a quote from an article repeated in larger type and set in a side column or a space where the main article flows around it

return on investment (ROI) – broadly, what you get back from your marketing (or any other) spend, so, the ratio of revenue to cost

salutation – the start of a personal communication, e.g. Dear Fred

search engine optimisation (SEO) – the process of designing and writing a website that gets high rankings on a search engine when a user types in relevant keywords

second person – the style of writing where the writer uses 'you'

sentence case – the "normal" way of writing a sentence, with the first word having a capital letter

sentence fragment – a sentence without a verb, e.g. Sentences must contain verbs. Or must they?

sitemap – a plan of a website used either purely as a planning aid at the design and copywriting stage or as a page on the finished site as a navigation aid for visitors

skyscraper - web advertisement running down the side of a web page or HTML email, deeper than it's wide

specifier – the individual involved in a buying decision who sets out the requirements for any given purchase

standfirst – the short paragraph or line of copy between the headline and the body of a magazine or newspaper article

strapline – an advertising slogan, usually attached to a logo, company or brand name

subhead – additional headline running under the main headline, often to add a point about an offer or free gift

superhead – a short introductory line that sits above the main headline

third person – the style of writing where the writer uses 'he', 'she', 'they' or 'it'

tip-on – any piece of card, paper or gift that is glued onto a magazine page

typeface – a particular design of letters, numbers and punctuation marks, such as Courier or Times New Roman, often used interchangeably with 'font'

white paper – article produced by an organisation to highlight its skills, experience or new thinking, usually offered as a download from a website. Differs from an article for publication in having a single source and being a plug for the author's company